COOKING WITH HOUGEN

COOKING
WITH
HOUGEN

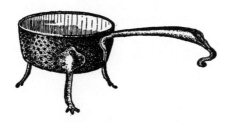

RICHARD T. HOUGEN

ABINGDON
NASHVILLE

COOKING WITH HOUGEN

ISBN 0-687-09679-0

Library of Congress Catalog Card Number: 60-9198

MANUFACTURED BY THE PARTHENON
PRESS, AT NASHVILLE, TENNESSEE,
UNITED STATES OF AMERICA

**To Cooks
Everywhere**

. . . and with grateful thanks to my wife, Mary, who has assisted me in preparing this cookbook

> "The discovery of a new dish
> does more for the happiness of man
> than the discovery of a new star."
>
> *Physiologie du Gout*
> Anthelme Brillat-Savarin

PREFACE

When a hotel manager is fortunate enough to have an unusually well-equipped kitchen, a fine co-operative staff, and above all thousands of wonderful guests who say, "Such delicious food—how do you do it?" Well, then one is inspired to create new recipes.

With today's accelerated way of life, the short cuts to finished food products, and the world being turned by man and woman power, we have forgotten the taste of "home cooked vittles." Gone are the days when there was an abundance of willing hands to grow the food and do the cooking; when each household boasted of plenty of butter, eggs, and cream in the springhouse. Yet, here are the remembrances of things past, set with different rules for mixing and planned for adaptation to our modern kitchens. The same foodstuffs as were used

7

for centuries are presented with different and original combinations in recipes of which you will say, "Here is real eating."

There is great pleasure derived in knowing that other folk approve of and come to use the recipes as a part of their everyday living. I hope you will find the contents stimulating, good eating, and fun to "stir up."

CONTENTS

9

BREAKFAST DISHES

BREAKFAST CINNAMON TOAST

1 TEASPOON CINNAMON
1 CUP WHITE SUGAR
1 BEATEN EGG

1. Mix the cinnamon and sugar.
2. Add the egg and blend.
3. Spread a generous tablespoonful of mixture on a slice of bread.
4. Bake bread for 15 minutes in a 400° F. oven.

This amount spreads about 10 slices. Crackling good.

CUSTARD OMELET

6 EGGS
2 TEASPOONS CHOPPED PARSLEY
4 TEASPOONS FINELY MINCED ONION
⅛ TEASPOON PEPPER
¼ TEASPOON SALT
1 CUP COFFEE CREAM OR RICH MILK

1. Beat eggs until light and creamy.
2. Add parsley, onion, pepper, salt, and cream. Mix.

3. Pour into 6 well-buttered custard cups. Fill each cup ¾ full.
4. Set custard cups in a pan of boiling water about 1 inch deep. Cover and keep water at a medium boil for 15 minutes.
5. Serve in the custard cups or turn out onto plates.

Serves 6.

EGGS A LA SUISSE

4 EGGS
2 TABLESPOONS BUTTER
SALT AND PEPPER
¼ CUP CREAM
½ CUP GRATED CHEESE

1. Rub butter over bottom of a casserole.
2. Sprinkle ¼ cup of grated cheese over butter.
3. Place eggs in casserole as you would for fried eggs.
4. Salt and pepper eggs.
5. Pour cream over eggs and sprinkle tops with the rest of the cheese.
6. Bake at 350° F. for 15 minutes.

Serves 2 or 4.

FRESH BLACKBERRY SYRUP

2 CUPS FRESH BLACK-
BERRIES
½ CUP WATER
½ CUP SUGAR

1. Boil berries and water for 10 minutes.
2. Strain and press through a sieve.
3. Add sugar to juice and pulp. Boil 5 to 8 minutes.
4. Serve hot or cold.

Makes 1 cup syrup for pancakes or ice cream topping.

The same recipe may be used for fresh blueberries, raspberries, cherries, or strawberries.

FROZEN RASPBERRY SYRUP

1 10 OZ. PACKAGE
FROZEN RASPBERRIES
½ CUP WATER
½ CUP SUGAR

1. Use the same method as for Fresh Blackberry Syrup.

Makes 1 cup of syrup for pancakes or ice cream topping.

14

NOTES

"Beautiful Soup, so rich and green,
Waiting in a hot tureen!"

Alice In Wonderland

Lewis Carroll

SOUPS

CREAM OF ONION SOUP

6 TABLESPOONS OLEO-
MARGARINE
4 TABLESPOONS FLOUR
4 CUPS MILK
2 CUPS CHICKEN STOCK
1 CUP CHOPPED ONIONS
½ TEASPOON SALT
¼ TEASPOON PEPPER
¼ CUP FINELY CUT GREEN
ONIONS
4 TABLESPOONS CREAM

1. Melt 2 tablespoons oleomargarine in top of double boiler. Add flour and mix well.
2. Add milk and chicken stock. Beat with wire whip to blend together and keep smooth.
3. Sauté onions in 4 tablespoons oleomargarine for 3 minutes. Add to soup mixture. Cook for 15 minutes.
4. Add salt, pepper, green onions, and cream. Mix and serve.

Serves 6.

CHILLED TOMATO BASQUE

1½ CUPS CANNED
    TOMATOES
3 CUPS TOMATO JUICE
¼ BAY LEAF
½ CUP FINELY MINCED
    CELERY
½ CUP FINELY MINCED
    ONION
½ TEASPOON CELERY SALT
    SALT AND PEPPER
1 TABLESPOON WORCES-
    TERSHIRE SAUCE

1. Drain tomatoes. Measure juice and add enough tomato juice to make the 3 cups.
2. Mix the first 5 ingredients. Simmer 15 minutes.
3. Remove bay leaf. Drain. Save liquid. Chop pulp exceedingly fine.
4. Add chopped pulp to liquid. Add celery salt, Worcestershire sauce, and salt and pepper to taste.
5. Chill until icy cold. Serve with a dab of the following:

1 CUP WHIPPED CREAM
1 TABLESPOON CHUTNEY
    PUREE

1 TABLESPOON CHOPPED
PARSLEY

a) Mix chutney and parsley with whipped cream.

Serves 6.

CLAM BISQUE

1 10 OZ. CAN MINCED
CLAMS
½ CUP FINELY CUT CELERY
3 TABLESPOONS OLEO-
MARGARINE
2 TABLESPOONS FLOUR
1 CUP MILK
CLAM JUICE (DRAINED
FROM CLAMS)
1 CUP CHICKEN STOCK OR
1 CHICKEN BOUILLON
CUBE DISSOLVED IN 1
CUP BOILING WATER
1 CUP MASHED POTATOES
¼ TEASPOON PEPPER
¼ TEASPOON SALT
1 TEASPOON CHOPPED
PARSLEY
1 TEASPOON GRATED RAW
CARROT

1. Drain clams. Save juice.
2. Sauté celery in 1 tablespoon oleomargarine for 5 minutes at medium low heat.
3. Melt 2 tablespoons oleomargarine in top of double boiler. Add flour and stir well with wire whip. Add milk gradually, stirring to keep smooth. Add clam juice and chicken stock.
4. Add potatoes and seasoning. Stir with wire whip to blend. Cook 5 minutes.
5. Add clams and celery. Stir. Cook 5 minutes.
6. Add parsley and carrots. Stir. Serve.

Serves 6.

CREOLE VEGETABLE SOUP

½ CUP BITE SIZE
    SPAGHETTI
¼ CUP CUT CELERY
1¼ CUPS ONIONS (CUT THE
    SAME SIZE AS CELERY)
¼ CUP CUT GREEN PEPPER
1 CUP CABBAGE (CUT THE
    SAME SIZE AS CELERY)
2 TABLESPOONS OLEO-
    MARGARINE
6 CUPS WATER
3 BEEF BOUILLON CUBES

3 CHICKEN BOUILLON
   CUBES
1 1 IB. CAN TOMATOES
1 BOX FROZEN MIXED
   GARDEN VEGETABLES
   (10 OZ. SIZE)
¼ TEASPOON PEPPER
¼ TEASPOON GARLIC SALT
½ TEASPOON SALT

1. Cook spaghetti as directed on package. Drain.
2. Sauté celery, onions, green pepper, and cabbage in oleomargarine on medium low heat for about 10 minutes, covered.
3. Bring water to a boil and dissolve the bouillon cubes in it.
4. Add tomatoes and frozen vegetables to bouillon. Bring to a boil and cook on medium heat for 10 minutes.
5. Add sautéed vegetables, garlic salt, pepper, salt, and spaghetti. Mix.

Serves 8 to 10.

FRESH MUSHROOM AND OYSTER STEW

1 10 OZ. CAN FROZEN
OYSTER STEW
2 CUPS SLICED FRESH
MUSHROOMS AND
STEMS
4 TABLESPOONS OLEO-
MARGARINE
1 CUP CHICKEN STOCK
2½ CUPS MILK
2 TABLESPOONS CHOPPED
PARSLEY
2 TABLESPOONS FINELY
CUT GREEN ONIONS
AND STEMS
½ CUP WHIPPED CREAM

1. Sauté mushrooms and stems in oleomargarine for 5 minutes.
2. Add chicken stock and simmer on medium low heat for 4 minutes.
3. Heat milk. Add frozen oyster stew. When stew has thawed remove oysters and chop fine. Return oysters to milk.
4. Mix mushrooms and chicken broth mixture with oyster stew.
5. Add parsley and onions. Bring to a boil.

6. Serve with a generous dab of whipped cream.

Serves 6 or only 4 if served as a luncheon soup with a sandwich and salad.

Quick, easy, nutritious, and delicious.

JELLIED TOMATO CONSOMME'

> 1 CUP TOMATO JUICE
> 1 TABLESPOON PLAIN
> GELATIN
> 1 CUP CHICKEN STOCK
> FEW CELERY LEAVES
> ½ BAY LEAF
> ¼ TEASPOON SALT
> ⅛ TEASPOON PEPPER
> ¼ TEASPOON CELERY SALT
> 1 TABLESPOON LEMON
> JUICE

1. Sprinkle gelatin over ¼ cup of the tomato juice. Allow to set for 10 minutes.
2. Bring the remaining tomato juice and chicken stock to a boil.
3. Add celery leaves, bay leaf, salt, pepper, and celery salt to the tomato juice and chicken stock. Bring to a boil.

4. Remove from the fire and strain. Add gelatin and tomato juice mixture to the strained liquid. Stir to dissolve gelatin. Add lemon juice. Stir.
5. Pour into oiled cups. Refrigerate until congealed.
6. Unmold congealed soup and serve with a dab of the following topping:

½ CUP COTTAGE CHEESE
¼ CUP WHIPPED CREAM
SALT AND PEPPER

a) Blend cottage cheese and whipped cream. Season with salt and pepper.

Serves 6.

POTAGE CHOUX FLEUR

2 CUPS MILK
1 PACKAGE FROZEN CAULI-FLOWER (8 OZ. SIZE)
1 CUP CHICKEN STOCK OR 2 CHICKEN BOUILLON CUBES DISSOLVED IN CUP BOILING WATER
½ BAY LEAF
1 CUP MASHED POTATOES
1 TABLESPOON FLOUR
¼ CUP MINCED ONION

1 TABLESPOON OLEO-
   MARGARINE
1 TABLESPOON CHOPPED
   PARSLEY
   SALT AND PEPPER, IF
   NEEDED

1. Boil 3 medium-sized potatoes. Drain off liquid. Save 1 cup of the liquid for the soup. Mash potatoes.
2. Mix flour with ½ cup cold chicken stock to form a paste. Add to the remaining stock. Cook for 3 minutes to thicken mixture in a double boiler. Stir in potato water.
3. Add milk and bay leaf. Cook for 15 minutes. Remove bay leaf.
4. Sauté the onions in the oleomargarine. Add onions and mashed potatoes to the soup. Whip with a wire whisk to break up potato lumps. Cook for 10 minutes.
5. Cook the cauliflower as directed on package. Drain and chop. Add to the soup. Cook for 10 minutes.
6. Add chopped parsley. Season with salt and pepper, if desired.

Serves 4 to 6.

NOTES

<blockquote>
"God sendeth and giveth both mouth and the meat."

Five Hundred Points of Good Husbandry
Thomas Tusser
</blockquote>

MEATS, FISH, POULTRY, AND ACCOMPANIMENTS

BAKED LAMB CHOPS, MONTEGO

12 LAMB CHOPS (2 CHOPS
    PER SERVING)
¾ CUP CORN BREAD
    CRUMBS
¾ CUP SOFT WHITE BREAD
    CRUMBS
⅛ TEASPOON SALT
⅛ TEASPOON PEPPER
¼ TEASPOON RUBBED SAGE
2 TABLESPOONS CAPERS
4 TABLESPOONS SLICED
    MUSHROOMS
9 TABLESPOONS CHICKEN
    BROTH
1 CUP CREAM
1 CUP WATER
2 TABLESPOONS FLOUR
    MIXED WITH ½ CUP
    COLD WATER
1 TABLESPOON CHOPPED
    PARSLEY
½ CUP OLEOMARGARINE

1. Split chops.
2. Mix corn bread and white bread crumbs with salt, pepper, sage, capers, mushrooms, and chicken broth.

3. Fill chops with dressing. Fasten with toothpicks.
4. Salt and pepper chops. Pat both sides with dry flour.
5. Brown chops in skillet, using oleomargarine.
6. Remove chops from skillet. Add ½ cup water to drippings. Cook for a few minutes, stirring all the time.
7. Place chops in baking dish. Pour sauce from skillet over chops. Cover. Bake at 350° F. for 1½ hours.
8. Remove chops. To make gravy add ½ cup water and the cold water and flour paste. Cook until gravy thickens. Stirring all the time.
9. Add cream. Cook to thicken. Season with salt and pepper. Add parsley.
10. Serve hot over lamp chops.

Serves 6.

BAKED PORK CHOPS, MANDARIN

4 CENTER-CUT PORK CHOPS
2 TABLESPOONS OLEO-MARGARINE
½ GREEN PEPPER
4 SLICES PINEAPPLE
3 TABLESPOONS CHOPPED SWEET PICKLE

½ CUP PINEAPPLE JUICE
½ CUP APPLE CIDER
½ CUP WATER
1 TEASPOON SUGAR
2 TABLESPOONS SOY
SAUCE
1 TABLESPOON CORN-
STARCH

1. Pat pork chops with flour and brown in a skillet with oleomargarine.
2. Remove chops to a casserole.
3. Add green pepper which has been cut in ¼ inch strips to drippings and sauté for 4 minutes.
4. Place a ring of pineapple on top of each chop. Place sautéed green pepper on pineapple. Sprinkle with chopped pickle.
5. Mix pineapple juice, cider, water, sugar, soy sauce, and cornstarch together. Cook in skillet used for browning chops until thick and clear. About 4 minutes.
6. Pour over chops. Bake in covered casserole for 1 hour at 375° F.

Serve with mounds of rice and the gravy.
This is easy to prepare and exotic in flavor.
Serves 4.

BAYOU SHRIMP BAKE

25 MEDIUM-SMALL, COOKED SHRIMPS
1 CUP QUICK-COOKING RICE
4 TABLESPOONS BUTTER
2 CUPS CANNED TOMATOES
1 CUP DRAINED SLICED MUSHROOMS (SAVE JUICE)
½ CUP WATER
¼ CUP CHOPPED STUFFED OLIVES
¼ CUP CHOPPED GREEN PEPPER
¼ CUP CHOPPED GREEN ONIONS, USING STEMS
¼ CUP CHOPPED PARSLEY
SALT AND PEPPER

1. Cut shrimps lengthwise.
2. Brown rice in skillet with 2 tablespoons butter. Cook on medium heat, stirring as rice browns. About 5 minutes.
3. Remove rice to a bowl and add tomatoes.
4. Sauté mushrooms in 2 tablespoons butter and ½ cup water for 5 minutes.

5. Mix rice with mushrooms. Add juice from mushrooms. Mix.
6. Add olives, onions, green pepper, and parsley. Mix. Add salt and pepper to taste.
7. Add shrimps. Mix.
8. Place in buttered casserole. Cover and bake at 350° F. for 45 minutes.

Serves 6. A most acceptable luncheon or supper dish with green salad.

BROILED TENDERLOIN STEAK ALAMO

6 BEEF TENDERLOIN STEAKS, 1½ INCH THICK
4 TABLESPOONS CATSUP
2 TABLESPOONS COOKING OIL
2 TABLESPOONS MINCED ONION
2 TABLESPOONS SOY SAUCE
3 STRIPS BACON

1. Mix catsup, oil, onion, and soy sauce to make a paste.
2. Cut bacon lengthwise to make 6 strips. Wrap a strip of bacon around each tenderloin steak and fasten with a toothpick.

3. Place steaks in buttered pan and spread half of the sauce over steaks.
4. Broil for 5 minutes. Turn and spread the remaining sauce on steaks. Broil for 5 minutes.

Serves 6.

CASSEROLE OF VEAL

1 LB. VEAL STEAK
3 TABLESPOONS OLEO-
MARGARINE
1 CUP CHICKEN BROTH
1 CUP WATER
½ TEASPOON SALT
⅛ TEASPOON PEPPER
3 TABLESPOONS FLOUR
½ CUP CANNED MUSH-
ROOMS, CUT UP
½ LB. EGG NOODLES
1 CUP BREAD CRUMBS
2 TABLESPOONS MELTED
OLEOMARGARINE

1. Cut veal into small cubes.
2. Flour meat lightly. Brown in oleomargarine.
3. Remove meat. Add chicken broth to drippings.
4. Drain liquid from mushrooms and use as part

of the 1 cup of water called for. Add flour, salt, and pepper. Mix well.

5. Add to chicken broth. Cook until gravy thickens. Stirring to avoid lumping. About 8 minutes.
6. Add mushrooms and veal. Mix.
7. Boil noodles in water as directed on package.
8. Drain noodles. Place in bottom of a well-greased casserole. Pour meat mixture over noodles.
9. Mix bread crumbs with melted oleomargarine and sprinkle over meat mixture.
10. Bake at 350° F. for 30 minutes. Then reduce heat to 300° F. and bake for 20 minutes longer.

Serves 6.

CHICKEN FLAKES WITH AVOCADO-NUT RING

10 CUPS WHITE BREAD
CUBES
5 CUPS CORN BREAD
CUBES
1 TEASPOON SALT
½ TEASPOON PEPPER
½ TEASPOON LEAF SAGE,
CRUMBLED
1 CUP CHOPPED ONIONS
4 TABLESPOONS OLEO-
MARGARINE
7½ OZ. FRESH WHOLE
MUSHROOMS
2 FIRM RIPE AVOCADOS
1 CUP CHOPPED PECANS
4½ CUPS CHICK STOCK
6 CUPS CHICKEN CREAM
SAUCE (PAGE 46)
5 CUPS CUBED COOKED
CHICKEN

1. Mix white bread and corn bread crumbs together.
2. Add salt, pepper, and sage and mix.
3. Sauté onions in 2 tablespoons oleomargarine for
4 minutes. Add to above mixture and mix.

41

4. Scrub mushroom caps and stems and rinse well in cold, salted water.
5. Cut off stems, peel stems, and cut in pieces. Sauté in pan after removing onions. Add stems to bread mixture.
6. Peel avocados and cut in cubes. Add cubed avocados and nuts to bread mixture. Mix.
7. Add chicken stock and mix well.
8. Sauté mushroom caps in 2 tablespoons oleomargarine on medium heat. Turn caps over to cook on both sides.
9. Grease a square or round angel food pan. Arrange mushroom caps, round side down, in a circle in bottom of pan. Cover with dressing and pack firmly.
10. Bake at 375° F. for 1 hour.
11. Prepare Chicken Cream Sauce. Add cubed chicken. Keep hot in double boiler until serving time.
12. When ring is baked, turn out on a platter. Serve cream chicken flakes in serving dish.
The dressing fills a 9½ inch tube pan.

Serves 8 to 10.

This elegant and easy to prepare dinner dish is acclaimed with "ohs" and "ahs."

CHICKEN ELSINORE

5 CUPS CHICKEN CREAM
   SAUCE (PAGE 46)
6 SERVINGS SLICED
   COOKED CHICKEN
5 OZ. PACKAGE EGG
   NOODLES
2 TABLESPOONS BUTTER
2 TABLESPOONS POPPY
   SEEDS
½ CUP TOASTED SLIVERED
   ALMONDS

1. Prepare Chicken Cream Sauce.
2. Place sliced chicken in sauce to heat.
3. Boil noodles in 3 quarts of salted, boiling water
   for 13 minutes. Drain well.
4. Add butter to noodles and turn carefully to mix
   as butter melts.
5. Fold in poppy seeds and almonds.
6. The chicken in cream sauce may be served over
   a mound of noodles or passed at the table in
   separate serving dishes.

Serves 6.

CHICKEN UPSIDE-DOWN CAKE

4 CUPS ½ INCH CUBED
COOKED CHICKEN
6 CUPS CHICKEN CREAM
SAUCE (PAGE 46)
6 TABLESPOONS OLEO-
MARGARINE
1¾ CUPS SIFTED FLOUR
1 CUP MILK
2 TEASPOONS BAKING
POWDER
2 EGGS, BEATEN
½ TEASPOON SALT

1. Beat oleomargarine until soft. Add eggs. Beat well.
2. Sift flour with baking powder and salt.
3. Add flour mixture to oleomargarine and eggs alternately with milk. Begin and end with flour.
4. Mix chicken with 4 cups of the chicken cream sauce and pour in a 9 x 12 baking pan. Pour batter over the top.
5. Bake at 375° F. for 45 minutes. Remove and turn upside down on a serving platter.
6. Cut in squares and serve with the remaining hot chicken cream sauce.

Serves 6 to 8.

CHICKEN PUFF

6 CUPS CHICKEN CREAM
SAUCE (PAGE 46)
½ CUP MELTED OLEO-
MARGARINE
½ CUP SIFTED FLOUR
4 EGG YOLKS, BEATEN
3 CUPS COOKED CHICKEN,
CUBED
2 TABLESPOONS MINCED
PARSLEY
1 CUP COOKED EGG
NOODLES
4 EGG WHITES, STIFFLY
BEATEN

1. Prepare Chicken Cream Sauce.
2. Mix oleomargarine and flour. Add to 4 cups of Cream Sauce. Cook in double boiler for 10 minutes.
3. Stir in egg yolks and cook 2 minutes.
4. Add cubed chicken, parsley, and noodles. Stir gently.
5. Remove from fire and carefully fold in stiffly beaten egg whites.
6. Turn into a well-greased spring mold with center ring or an angel food pan which has a large center ring. Place mold in a pan with hot water, about 1 inch deep.

7. Bake at 375° F. for 1 to 1 ½ hours or until a knife blade comes out clean when inserted.
8. Turn out onto a platter and serve with the following sauce:

> **2 CUPS CHICKEN CREAM SAUCE**
> **1 CUP SLICED SAUTEED MUSHROOMS**
> **1 CUP CUT CASHEW NUTS**

a) Mix mushrooms and nuts with the hot sauce.

This puff makes 10 slices.
Ideal for luncheon or buffets.

CHICKEN CREAM SAUCE

> **½ CUP CHICKEN FAT**
> **1 CUP FLOUR**
> **6 CUPS CHICKEN STOCK**
> **SALT AND PEPPER**

1. Melt chicken fat in double boiler. Stir in flour. Cook for 5 minutes, stirring constantly to prevent sticking.
2. Heat chicken stock. Add to the above, stirring constantly while cooking for 10 minutes to thicken.
3. Season to taste.

Makes 6 cups.

HAM LOAF

1½ LBS. PORK GROUND
WITH ½ LB. HAM
1 TABLESPOON CHOPPED
CHIVES
½ CUP FINE CRACKER
CRUMBS
¼ TEASPOON PEPPER
½ TEASPOON SALT
2 EGGS
1 4 OZ. CAN PIMIENTO
1 CUP MASHED POTATOES
¼ CUP MILK
2 TABLESPOONS SESAME
SEEDS

1. Drain pimiento and force through a sieve.
2. Add to the meat with the rest of the ingredients, except sesame seeds. Mix well.
3. Place in a loaf pan and round off the top. Sprinkle with sesame seeds.
4. Bake at 375° F. for 1½ hours.
5. Serve hot or cold.

Serves 6 to 8.

MARAZELLA HAM AND BEEF ROLL

12 SLICES HAM (2½ OUNCE
    SIZE)
12 SLICES BEEF ROUND
    (2½ OUNCE SIZE)
¾ CUP FLOUR
 1 TABLESPOON PEPPER
 1 TABLESPOON SALT
 1 CUP FAT
 1 CUP WATER

1. Lay a slice of ham on a slice of beef. Roll up as for jelly roll. Secure with toothpicks. Cover each roll well by rolling in mixture of flour, salt, and pepper.
2. Heat fat in skillet and brown each roll carefully.
3. Remove to a casserole. Add 1 cup water to drippings in skillet. Bring to a boil and pour over meat.
4. Bake at 375° F. for 1 ½ hours.
5. Remove rolls and make gravy by mixing 4 tablespoons flour with 1 cup water to form a smooth paste. Add to drippings. Cook for 10 minutes, stirring to keep smooth.
6. Serve some gravy over each roll.

Serves 12.

LOBSTER-SCALLOP HALFSHELL

6 FLORIDA LOBSTER TAILS
(7 TO 8 OZ. SIZE)
1 CUP CUBED COOKED
SCALLOPS
6 TABLESPOONS OLEO-
MARGARINE
5 TABLESPOONS FLOUR
½ TEASPOON SALT
½ TEASPOON PEPPER
2 CUPS MILK
1 CUP CREAM
½ CUP SLICED MUSHROOMS
3 EGG YOLKS, BEATEN
2 HARD-COOKED EGGS,
CHOPPED
2 TEASPOONS CHOPPED
PARSLEY
1 CUP BUTTERED BREAD
CRUMBS
PAPRIKA

1. Boil lobster tails. Remove meat and cut into cubes. Wash shells and save for filling.
2. Melt 4 tablespoons oleomargarine in top of double boiler. Add flour, salt, and pepper. Cook 5 minutes.
3. Add milk and cream. Cook until sauce thickens. Stir frequently.

4. Sauté mushrooms in 2 tablespoons of oleomargarine. Add lobster meat to mushrooms. Stir together and cook for 3 minutes on low heat.
5. Add egg yolks to thickened sauce. Cook 3 minutes. Stir to keep smooth.
6. Add lobster, mushrooms, hard-cooked eggs, scallops, and parsley to sauce. Mix.
7. Fill each lobster shell with this mixture. Sprinkle tops with buttered bread crumbs. Sprinkle with paprika.
8. Place filled shells in a baking pan. Bake at 400° F. for 15 minutes.
9. The remaining sauce is kept hot in double boiler. Serve a spoonful over one end of each lobster at serving time.

6 generous servings.

VARIATIONS:
   a) Use only lobster meat.
   b) Use cream sauce base with crabmeat flakes. Place mixture in a casserole or individual ramekins to bake.

POULET DORE (GOLDEN CHICKEN)

1 FRYER, CUT INTO SERV-
ING PIECES
6 TABLESPOONS CHOPPED
ALMONDS
1½ CUPS CRUSHED GRAPE-
NUTS FLAKES
1½ TEASPOONS CELERY
SEED
½ TEASPOON SALT
¼ TEASPOON PEPPER
¼ TEASPOON GARLIC SALT
4 TABLESPOONS CHOPPED
PARSLEY
1 EGG, BEATEN
2 TABLESPOONS MILK
½ CUP PANCAKE MIX
4 TABLESPOONS OLEO-
MARGARINE

1. Steam chicken for ½ hour. This can accomplished by placing chicken in a sieve over boiling water. Cover and allow to steam.
2. Mix almonds, Grapenuts Flakes, celery seed, salt, pepper, garlic salt, and parsley together.
3. Mix egg with milk.
4. While chicken is hot coat each piece with dry pancake mix.

5. Then dip in egg wash and finish rolling in the Grapenuts mixture.
6. Melt oleomargarine in a casserole. Place chicken in one layer only. Cover and bake at 375° F. for 45 minutes.

This crispy crunchy baked chicken is delicious and unusual.

OYSTER RAMEKIN

1 12 OZ. CAN FROZEN OYSTERS OR 1½ CUPS FRESH OYSTERS
1 TABLESPOON OLEO-MARGARINE
2 TABLESPOONS FLOUR
1 CUP CREAM
¼ TEASPOON SALT
⅛ TEASPOON PEPPER
1 TABLESPOON CHOPPED PARSLEY
2 BEATEN EGG YOLKS
½ CUP FRESH BREAD CRUMBS
1 TABLESPOON MELTED OLEOMARGARINE

1. Thaw, drain, and chop oysters.
2. Melt oleomargarine in top of double boiler.
3. Stir in flour and mix well.
4. Add cream. Stir and cook until thickened.
5. Add salt, pepper, parsley, and egg yolks. Mix well.
6. Add oysters. Mix.
7. Fill 4 buttered ramekins. Mix melted oleomargarine with bread crumbs and sprinkle over oyster mixture.
8. Bake at 400° F. for 15 minutes in a pan of hot water.

Serves 4.

ROLLED BEEF ROUND, CHEESE DRESSING

2 IB. SLICED BEEF ROUND, ½ INCH THICK
2½ CUPS FRESH BREAD CUBES
¼ TEASPOON SAGE
¼ TEASPOON PEPPER
½ TEASPOON SALT
½ CUP BEEF BOUILLON
1 CUP GRATED AMERICAN CHEESE
6 MEDIUM-SMALL TART APPLES

1. Mix the bread cubes, seasonings, and bouillon.
2. Add grated cheese and mix.
3. Spread over the beef slice and roll as for a jelly roll. Pin together with 2 or 3 toothpicks.
4. Salt and pepper the beef roll. Dot with oleomargarine.
5. Place about 2 tablespoons of oleomargarine in bottom of small roasting pan, then the meat roll.
6. Place uncovered in a 400° F. oven for 20 minutes to brown. Cover and bake 1 hour and 40 minutes longer.
7. During the last hour of baking add whole, unpeeled apples and bake along with the meat.
8. Slice the round of beef and serve a baked apple with each serving.

Serves 6.

SAVOY RICE

2 TABLESPOONS OLEO-
MARGARINE
1 CUP QUICK-COOKING
RICE
1 CUP CHICKEN STOCK OR
USE 1 CHICKEN BOUIL-
LON CUBE DISSOLVED IN
CUP WATER
¾ CUP FINELY DICED
BAKED HAM
1 4 OZ. CAN MUSHROOMS,
DRAINED (SAVE JUICE)
½ CUP MINCED GREEN
PEPPER
½ CUP FINELY MINCED
ONION
¼ CUP FINELY MINCED
PIMIENTO

1. Melt oleomargarine in skillet. Add rice and stir until brown.
2. Add chicken stock and juice from drained mush-rooms. Mix. Cover and cook on very low heat until rice absorbs all the liquid.
3. Add ham and mushrooms. Cover and cook 5 min-utes. Turn rice with with fork occasionally to prevent sticking.
4. Add green pepper, onions, pimiento, and cook covered 5 minutes longer on low heat.

Serves 6.

Savoy Rice makes an excellent luncheon dish.

SMOTHERED VEAL CHOPS

4 VEAL CHOPS, ½ INCH
  THICK
½ CUP BREAD CRUMBS
SALT AND PEPPER
HOT WATER
4 TEASPOONS OLEO-
  MARGARINE

1. Salt and pepper chops.
2. Press bread crumbs onto both sides of the chops.
3. Place chops in a baking pan and dot with oleo-margarine.
4. Pour ¼ cup of hot water around chops.
5. Place in 350° F. oven to bake uncovered for 1 hour. Add 2 or 3 tablespoons of water as baking continues if there is no moisture. The amount of fat on chops determines whether you need this extra water to keep chops from sticking to pan.

4 servings.

A much preferred method to achieve breaded veal chops. Easy, quick and really tasty crumb coating. Pork chops are also excellent prepared in this manner.

SOUTHERN FRIED CHICKEN

1 FRYER, CUT IN SERVING
  PIECES
½ CUP PANCAKE MIX
  SALT AND PEPPER
1 EGG, BEATEN
2 TABLESPOONS MILK
  DEEP FAT FOR FRYING

1. Steam chicken for 20 minutes. This can be accomplished by placing chicken in a sieve over boiling water. Cover and allow to steam.
2. Mix salt and pepper into pancake mix.
3. Beat egg and milk together.
4. Dip the chicken in egg mixture then roll in pancake mix until pieces are well coated.
5. Heat fat and fry chicken until golden brown.

SOUTHERN HASH

½ CUP DICED ONION
½ CUP DICED GREEN
PEPPER
2 TABLESPOONS OLEOMAR-
GARINE
2 CUPS COOKED ROAST
BEEF, CUBED
2 CUPS CANNED
TOMATOES
1 CUP DICED RAW
POTATOES
2 TEASPOONS SALT
¼ TEASPOON PEPPER
⅛ TEASPOON GARLIC SALT

1. Sauté onions and green pepper in oleomargarine for 3 minutes.
2. Add all other ingredients and cook on medium heat for 20 minutes or until potatoes are tender. Cover skillet for the first 15 minutes of cooking then remove cover until hash is cooked.

Serves 4.

SWORDFISH STEAK

4 SWORDFISH STEAKS, ½
INCH THICK
4 TABLESPOONS BUTTER
2 LEMONS
2 CUPS WATER
SALT AND PEPPER

1. Place fish in a baking pan. Dot each steak with 1 tablespoon butter. Sprinkle with salt and pepper.
2. Place three thin slices of lemon on top of each steak.
3. Pour the water into the pan.
4. Place in a 375° F. oven and bake for 30 minutes.
5. Turn on top burner of oven to broil for 5 minutes.

Serves 4.

TURKEY FLAKES WITH RICE CUSTARD

6 CUPS CHICKEN CREAM
SAUCE (PAGE 46. USE
TURKEY BROTH IN PLACE
OF CHICKEN BROTH TO
MAKE SAUCE)

6 CUPS COOKED TURKEY
CUT IN LARGE CUBES
1 CUP QUICK-COOKING
RICE
1 CUP CHICKEN BROTH
½ TEASPOON SALT
½ TEASPOON PEPPER
1 PINT MILK
3 EGGS

1. Make sauce in double boiler. Place turkey in sauce and heat thoroughly.
2. Cook rice in chicken broth per directions given on rice package.
3. Scald milk. Add to slightly beaten eggs, mixing with a wire whip as you add hot milk.
4. Add salt and pepper. Mix.
5. Fill buttered custard cups 1/3 full of rice. Add enough custard to fill cups. Place custard cups in a pan with enough hot water to cover bottom of pan.
6. Bake at 325° F. for 1 hour.
7. Unmold custard and serve with hot turkey flakes over it.

Serves 12.

Creamed chicken flakes will do just as nicely.

BEET RELISH

1 1 LB. 1 OZ. CAN BEETS
½ CUP SUGAR
¾ CUP CIDER VINEGAR
¼ CUP WATER
4 TABLESPOONS CINNA-
MON CANDY
6 WHOLE CLOVES
1 SMALL STICK CINNAMON

1. Drain beets. Chop very fine.
2. Combine all other ingredients and boil 15 minutes. Remove cinnamon stick.
3. Add beets to the hot liquid and mix well.
4. Refrigerate before serving.

CINNAMON APPLE SLICES

2 TART APPLES
1 CUP SUGAR
2¾ CUPS WATER
1/3 CUP RED CINNAMON
CANDY
½ TEASPOON RED FOOD
COLORING

61

1. Boil sugar, water, and cinnamon candy for 5 minutes.
2. Add food coloring. Stir.
3. Cut unpeeled apples into eighths. Boil in syrup until apples become transparent. About 15 minutes. Turn apple sections while cooking.
4. Remove from syrup and cool.

DEVONSHIRE COUNTRY RELISH

1½ CUPS MINCEMEAT
½ CUP CHOPPED APPLES
1 CUP CHOPPED SWEET PICKLES
3 CUPS WHOLE-KERNEL CANNED CORN
½ CUP SWEET PICKLE JUICE (DRAINED FROM PICKLES)

1. Drain corn.
2. Mix all ingredients together.
3. Simmer at medium heat for 15 minutes.
4. Chill and serve on relish tray.

Yields 6 cups relish.

MINTED APPLE RINGS

1 CUP SUGAR
2¾ CUPS WATER
⅛ TEASPOON GREEN FOOD
COLORING
2 TEASPOONS MINT
FLAVORING
2 TART MEDIUM-SIZE
APPLES

1. Mix sugar, water, and food coloring in a heavy skillet. Boil for 5 minutes.
2. Slice unpeeled apples crosswise about ¼ inch thick. Do not core apples, but remove seeds with knife point.
3. Add mint flavoring to syrup.
4. Place apple slices in syrup. Boil at medium heat for 15 to 20 minutes or until apples become transparent. Turn slices occasionally and baste with syrup.
5. Remove slices from syrup and cool.

Makes about 12 apples slices to serve with Roast Lamb or Grilled Lamb Chops. The remaining sauce may be used for a Clear Mint Sundae Topping.

SANDALWOOD JELLY

3 CUPS TOMATOES, CUT
IN SECTIONS (ABOUT 4
MEDIUM TOMATOES)
1 ORANGE, CUT IN SLICES
1 LEMON, CUT IN SLICES
2 LIMES, CUT IN SLICES
⅛ TEASPOON MACE
¼ TEASPOON NUTMEG
4 CUPS SUGAR
1 BOX FRUIT PECTIN

1. Mix tomatoes, fruit, and spices with 1 cup water. Cook until fruit is soft. About 20 minutes.
2. Put through a food mill or sieve. Yields about 3 cups.
3. Return juice to stove and bring to a rolling boil.
4. Mix sugar and fruit pectin. Add to the boiling juice. Bring to a rolling boil and boil for 1 minute. Stir constantly.
5. Remove from heat and pour into jelly glasses.

Makes 6 glasses of jelly.
Excellent meat accompaniment.

NOTES

NOTES

POTATOES AND VEGETABLES

BROWNED BUTTER RICE

¼ CUP OLEOMARGARINE
1 CUP QUICK-COOKING
RICE
1 CUP CHICKEN STOCK
OR USE 1 CHICKEN
BOUILLON CUBE WITH
1 CUP OF BOILING
WATER
SALT TO TASTE

1. Melt and brown oleomargarine in skillet.
2. Add rice and stir until all grains are coated with oleomargarine.
3. Slowly add chicken stock. Season and stir. Cover and set rice on simmer for 20 minutes.

This rice is used in the preparation of Tossed Salad Indonesia (Page 106).

Browned Butter Rice is very good served with Creamed Chicken.

CRYSTAL GINGER SWEET POTATOES

4 MEDIUM-SIZE SWEET
POTATOES
3 TABLESPOONS BUTTER
1/3 CUP CRYSTALIZED
GINGER CUT INTO
SMALL PIECES
½ CUP ORANGE JUICE
¼ CUP BROWN SUGAR,
FIRMLY PACKED

1. Cook peeled sweet potatoes. Cut in slices. This can be done before or after cooking.
2. Arrange a layer of sliced potatoes in a buttered casserole. Dot with butter and sprinkle with ginger. Repeat with the next layer.
3. Pour orange juice over potatoes and sprinkle with brown sugar.
4. Bake uncovered at 375° F. for 45 minutes. Baste occasionally to keep moist.

Serves 6.

CAPER HASHED POTATOES

2 CUPS CUBED, COOKED
POTATOES
¼ CUP CAPERS
¼ CUP CHOPPED GREEN
PEPPER
½ CUP FINELY CHOPPED
GREEN ONIONS AND
TOPS
½ TEASPOON SALT
½ TEASPOON PEPPER
¼ CUP MELTED OLEO-
MARGARINE
PAPRIKA
2 TABLESPOONS CHOPPED
PARSLEY

1. Mix all ingredients except paprika and parsley together.
2. Place in baking pan and sprinkle with paprika.
3. Bake at 500° F. for 20 minutes. Turn with pancake turner as top of potatoes brown.
4. Just before serving stir in parsley.

6 servings of potatoes with a tangy flavor.

NEW POTATOES
WITH SAFFRON CREAM

6 BOILED NEW POTATOES
3 TABLESPOONS BOILING
WATER
¼ TEASPOON SAFFRON
2 TABLESPOONS OLEO-
MARGARINE
2 TABLESPOONS FLOUR
1 CUP MILK
¼ TEASPOON SALT
⅛ TEASPOON PEPPER
CHOPPED PARSLEY

1. Pour boiling water over saffron and allow to stand until sauce is finished.
2. While potatoes are boiling make sauce.
3. Melt oleomargarine in top of double boiler. Add flour. Mix well.
4. Slowly add milk beating with wire whip to keep smooth. Cook until thickened.
5. Add salt and pepper. Mix.
6. Strain saffron liquid into sauce. Mix.
7. Serve over boiled potatoes. Sprinkle with chopped parsley.

Serves 6.

SEVILLE SWEET POTATOES

⅛ CUP ORANGE JUICE
4 HALF ORANGE SHELLS
½ CUP MINCEMEAT
2 TABLESPOONS BUTTER
4 MARSHMALLOWS
1 CUP MASHED SWEET POTATOES (3 MEDIUM POTATOES)

1. Cut three oranges in half and squeeze out the juice. Remove pulp from orange shell.
2. Peel and boil sweet potatoes until tender when pierced with a fork. Drain well and mash. Use only 1 cup.
3. Heat orange juice, add butter then beat into the mashed potatoes.
4. Mix in the mincemeat.
5. Pile the mixture into orange shells and place in a baking pan. Pour a little water in bottom of pan to keep oranges from sticking. Bake in a 400° F. oven for 10 minutes.
6. Remove from oven and press a marshmallow in each.
7. Return to oven to toast marshmallow.

4 servings of sweet potatoes in a delightful tasty setting.

74

NUTMEG SWEET POTATOES

6 MEDIUM-SIZE SWEET
POTATOES, COOKED
2 TABLESPOONS OLEO-
MARGARINE
¼ CUP DARK CORN SYRUP
1 CUP BROWN SUGAR
1 TEASPOON FRESHLY
GRATED NUTMEG

1. Cut potatoes in slices.
2. Melt oleomargarine and mix with syrup and sugar.
3. Arrange potatoes in greased baking dish or casserole.
4. Spread sugar mixture over tops of potatoes. Sprinkle nutmeg over sugar mixture.
5. Bake at 375° F. for 20 or 30 minutes.
6. Spoon sauce over each serving of potatoes.

Serves 6.

SHREDDED POTATO PATTY

2 CUPS SHREDDED COLD
COOKED POTATOES
¼ CUP FINELY CHOPPED
ONION

¼ TEASPOON SALT
⅛ TEASPOON PEPPER
2 TABLESPOONS OLEO-
MARGARINE

1. Mix first 4 ingredients together with a fork.
2. Shape into desired size patties and brown on both
   sides in oleomargarine.

Serves 4.

SPICED SWEET POTATOES

2 CUPS HOT MASHED
SWEET POTATOES
⅛ TEASPOONS CLOVES
½ TEASPOON MACE
¼ TEASPOON ALLSPICE
⅛ TEASPOON GROUND
CARDAMON
⅛ TEASPOON NUTMEG
½ TEASPOON CINNAMON
⅛ TEASPOON SALT
¼ CUP HOT APPLE CIDER
2 TABLESPOONS OLEO-
MARGARINE

1. Heat cider with all the spices and salt. Add oleomargarine.

2. Add hot liquid to potatoes and whip together.
3. Bake in well-buttered casserole, covered, at 375°
   F. for 20 minutes.

Serves 6.

BRAISED CELERY

3 CUPS CELERY, CUT
THINLY CROSSWISE
2 TABLESPOONS COOKING
OIL
SALT AND PEPPER

1. Place cut celery in cold water to make crisp.
2. Drain lightly.
3. Heat oil in skillet and toss in celery. Season to taste. Cover and cook on medium heat for about 10 minutes. Stir occasionally and add a little water if necessary to keep from scorching.

Serves 4.

CARROT PUDDING

2 CUPS COOKED CARROTS
2 CUPS SCALDED MILK
1 TABLESPOON SUGAR
½ TEASPOON SALT
¼ TEASPOON PEPPER
2 TABLESPOONS FLOUR
3 EGGS, BEATEN
2 TABLESPOONS MELTED
OLEOMARGARINE

1. Put cooked carrots through sieve or food mill.
2. Add hot milk. Mix.
3. Mix sugar with salt, pepper, and flour. Add to above mixture.
4. Add eggs. Mix.
5. Add oleomargarine. Mix.
6. Place in buttered ramekins or casserole. Bake at 350° F. for 30 minutes.

Serves 10.

CAULIFLOWER PARMESAN

1 CAULIFLOWER HEAD,
SEPARATED INTO 12
CAULIFLOWERETTES
½ CUP BREAD CRUMBS
½ CUP GRATED PARMESAN
CHEESE
1 EGG
1 TABLESPOON MILK
2 TABLESPOONS MELTED
OLEOMARGARINE

1. Cook cauliflowerettes for 7 minutes in salted water. Drain.
2. Mix bread crumbs with cheese.
3. Beat egg with milk.
4. Dip each cauliflowerette in egg wash, then in crumb mixture.
5. Arrange in a buttered casserole. Pour melted oleo-margarine over cauliflowerettes.
6. Cover. Bake at 350° F. for 20 minutes.

Serves 6.

CRANBERRY BEETS

1 CUP SUGAR
1 CUP WATER
2 CUPS RAW CRANBERRIES
1 TEASPOON CORNSTARCH
1 TABLESPOON COLD
  WATER
1 NO. 303 CAN CUBED
  BEETS

1. Mix water and sugar and boil for 5 minutes.
2. Add washed cranberries and cook without stirring until cranberries pop open. About 5 minutes.
3. Drain juice from cranberries. Return juice to heat.
4. Mix cornstarch with cold water to make a smooth paste. Add to juice. Cook until clear and thickened. About 3 to 4 minutes.
5. Add berries and drained beets to thickened juice. Heat all together until hot.
   If you use whole or sliced beets, cut into cubes.

Serves 8.

Hot or cold, these beets have a delicious flavor.

HEARTS OF ARTICHOKES FONDUE

1 PACKAGE OF FROZEN
ARTICHOKE HEARTS
1 CUP CREAM SAUCE
(PAGE 82)
½ CUP SWISS CHEESE, CUT
IN SMALL PIECES
DASH OF POULTRY
SEASONING
½ CUP BREAD CRUMBS
MIXED WITH 2 TABLE-
SPOONS MELTED BUTTER

1. Place frozen artichoke hearts in a sauce pan with 1 cup of water and ½ teaspoon salt. Cover and bring to a boil. Remove from fire and allow to stand covered 15 minutes.
2. Drain artichoke hearts and place in buttered casserole. Pour the cream sauce over the vegetables and sprinkle with cheese. Shower the buttered bread crumbs over the top. Sprinkle over all a bit of poultry seasoning.
3. Bake at 350° F. for 30 minutes.

Mild and delicate. Serves 4.

CREAM SAUCE

2 TABLESPOONS SIFTED
  FLOUR
2 TABLESPOONS BUTTER
1 CUP RICH MILK
¼ TEASPOON SALT
⅛ TEASPOON PEPPER

1. Melt butter, add flour and stir while cooking for 3 minutes in a double boiler.
2. Heat milk. Add to mixture in double boiler. Continue stirring while cooking for 5 minutes.
3. Season with above amounts of salt and pepper or to taste.

Makes 1 cup of cream sauce.

PINEAPPLE BEETS

2 TABLESPOONS CORN-
STARCH
1 CUP PINEAPPLE JUICE
½ CUP SUGAR
¼ CUP CIDER VINEGAR
1 TABLESPOON OLEOMAR-
GARINE
1 NO. 303 CAN BEETS
½ CUP CRUSHED PINEAPPLE

1. Stir cornstarch into ½ cup of the pineapple juice to make a smooth paste.
2. Add remaining pineapple juice, sugar, and vinegar. Stir.
3. Place in a double boiler. Cook until thickened and clear. About 8 minutes. Stir often to prevent lumping.
4. Add oleomargarine and crushed pineapple.
5. Drain beets. Cut in sections and add to the above.
6. Heat well. Serve.

Serves 6 to 8.

SPANISH EGGPLANT

2 CUPS EGGPLANT, CUBED
½ CUP CUT CELERY
½ CUP CUT ONIONS
¼ CUP CUT GREEN PEPPER
¼ CUP OLEOMARGARINE
½ TEASPOON SALT
¼ TEASPOON PEPPER
1 CUP TOMATOES

1. Soak cubed eggplant in salt water for 10 minutes.
2. Sauté onions, celery, and green pepper in oleo-margarine.
3. Add tomatoes, salt, pepper, and eggplant and cook covered for 20 to 25 minutes on medium heat.

Serves 6.

SPINACH SOUFFLE'

2 PACKAGES FROZEN
CHOPPED SPINACH
2 TABLESPOONS CHOPPED
ONION
2 TABLESPOONS OLEOMAR-
GARINE

1 CUP SOFT BREAD
CRUMBS
1 CUP CREAM SAUCE
(PAGE 82)
3 EGG YOLKS
½ TEASPOON SALT
¼ TEASPOON PEPPER
⅛ TEASPOON PAPRIKA
3 STIFFLY BEATEN EGG
WHITES

1. Cook spinach as directed on package. Drain well.
2. Sauté onions in oleomargarine.
3. Add onions and bread crumbs to spinach. Mix.
4. Combine the above with cream sauce.
5. Add egg yolks. Beat well.
6. Add seasonings. Mix.
7. Gently fold in egg whites.
8. Pour into a well-buttered casserole and set in a pan of water.
9. Bake at 350° F. for 35 to 40 minutes.

Serves 8 to 10.

VEGETABLE GUMBO

½ 10 OZ. PACKAGE FROZEN
WHOLE SMALL OKRA
½ 10 OZ. PACKAGE FROZEN
CORN
1 I LB. CAN TOMATOES
½ CUP QUICK-COOKING
RICE
¼ TEASPOON PEPPER
½ TEASPOON SALT
⅛ TEASPOON CELERY SALT
3 TABLESPOONS OLEOMAR-
GARINE
¼ CUP WATER
1 CUP FRESH BREAD CUBES

1. In a buttered casserole place frozen okra, then frozen corn.
2. Sprinkle seasoning over vegetables.
3. Sprinkle rice over the above mixture.
4. Break up tomatoes and pour over rice.
5. Dot with oleomargarine and add water.
6. Top with bread cubes.
7. Bake covered at 375° F. for ½ hour. Uncover. Broil for a few minutes to brown bread cubes.

Serves 6.

655-8394
1500

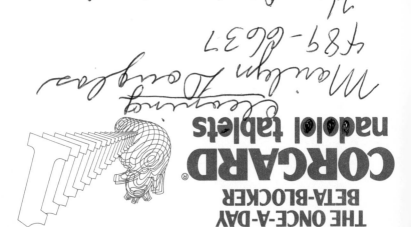

THE ONCE-A-DAY
BETA-BLOCKER
CORGARD®
nadolol tablets

Marilyn Douglas
484-6637
Yes can
Wants for Rent

NOTES

NOTES

SALADS
AND SANDWICHES

BOYSENBERRY SALAD, SANTA ANA

1 PACKAGE BLACK RASP-
  BERRY GELATIN
1 1 LB. CAN BOYSEN-
  BERRIES
¾ CUP WATER
2 TABLESPOONS VINEGAR
2 CUPS FINELY SHREDDED
  CABBAGE

1. Drain berries. Add water to juice. Bring to a boil.
2. Add hot juice to gelatin. Stir to dissolve. Add vinegar. Mix.
3. Refrigerate until slightly congealed.
4. Fold in berries and cabbage.
5. Pour into well-oiled 8 x 8 inch pan. Refrigerate to set.
6. Cut into portions. Serve on lettuce leaf. Top with Whipped Cream Dressing. (Page 110.)

Serves 12.

CELERY-WALNUT SALAD

1 CUP WALNUTS
2 CUPS CELERY, CUT IN 1
INCH PIECES
1 TABLESPOON GRATED
ORANGE RIND
1 TABLESPOON CHOPPED
PARSLEY
FRENCH DRESSING

1. Boil walnuts in water for 10 minutes.
2. Chill in ice water and dry on a towel.
3. Mix walnuts, celery, orange rind, and parsley.
4. Mix with French dressing and chill for 30 minutes.

Serves 6.

CHICKEN SALAD SCHEHERAZADE

1 CUP CUBED COOKED
CHICKEN
½ CUP CUT TOASTED
BRAZIL NUTS
½ CUP FINELY CUT CELERY
½ CUP SLICE MUSHROOMS
1 TEASPOON LEMON JUICE

½ TEASPOON GRATED
LEMON RIND
1 CUP CUBED AVOCADO
1 CUP MAYONNAISE
SALT AND PEPPER TO
TASTE
SHREDDED LETTUCE OR
GREENS
3 TOMATOES
½ CUP CHOPPED TOASTED
BRAZIL NUTS

1. Combine the first 8 ingredients and season with salt and pepper.
2. Arrange shredded lettuce on 4 individual salad plates. Place 5 small sections of tomato to form a circle on each mound of lettuce or greens.
3. Place a serving of salad in the center of each tomato ring.
4. Top each salad with a generous amount of the ½ cup of chopped, toasted brazil nuts.

4 luncheon size servings of salad. A variety of breads and a glamorous relish tray makes this a fine one course meal.

DRESSED EGGS

1 TEASPOON DRY
MUSTARD
2 TABLESPOONS SALAD OIL
2 TABLESPOONS CIDER
VINEGAR
1 TEASPOON SALT
¼ TEASPOON PEPPER
1 TEASPOON FINELY
MINCED ONION
1 TEASPOON ANCHOVY
PASTE
6 HARD-BOILED EGGS
½ CUP SIEVED BOILED
POTATOES
PAPRIKA
12 CAPERS

1. Mix mustard, oil, vinegar, salt, pepper, onion, and anchovy paste.
2. Cut eggs in half lengthwise. Remove yolks and force through a sieve.
3. Add sieved potatoes and yolks to first mixture. Beat well.
4. Stuff egg halves with mixture. About 1 heaping teaspoon per half egg.
5. Sprinkle with paprika and top with a caper.

Makes 12 stuffed egg halves.

Makes an attractive salad plate using 3 egg halves alternated with 2 tomato wedges around a center mound of cole slaw.

PIQUANT SALAD

1 PACKAGE LEMON
  GELATIN
2 CUPS BOILING WATER
½ CUP FINELY SLICED
  RADISHES
½ CUP CUT UP GREEN
  PEPPER
1 CUP SHREDDED SAUER-
  KRAUT THAT HAS BEEN
  CUT UP

1. Dissolve gelatin in boiling water. Refrigerate until it begins to congeal.
2. Stir in radishes, pepper, and sauerkraut.
3. Spoon into well-oiled pan. Refrigerate until set.
4. Cut into portions and serve with Whipped Cream Dressing.

Serves 6 to 8.

CHICKEN AND OYSTER SALAD IN TOMATO ROSETTE

6 RIPE TOMATOES,
MEDIUM SIZE
1½ CUPS SAUTEED OYSTERS
(CUT IN PIECES)
1 CUP COOKED CHICKEN
(CUT IN CUBES)
1 CUP CUBED CELERY
(CUT THE SIZE OF
CHICKEN CUBES)
2 TEASPOONS LEMON
JUICE
1½ CUPS WHIPPED CREAM
DRESSING (PAGE 110)
SALT AND PEPPER
POTATO CHIPS
SPICED PEAR HALVES

1. Cut tomatoes into rosettes.
2. Prepare oysters and cool.
3. Mix oysters, chicken, celery, lemon juice, and dressing. Season to taste.
4. Fill tomatoes and place on lettuce leaf. Garnish with potato chips and spiced pear.

Serves 6.

GARNET SALAD

1 CUP CANNED OR FRESH-
LY COOKED RHUBARB
1 PACKAGE STRAWBERRY
GELATIN
½ CUP SWEET PICKLES,
CUT UP
½ CUP FINELY CUT CELERY
ORANGE JUICE

1. Drain rhubarb. Measure rhubarb juice and add enough orange juice to make 2 cups.
2. Bring juice to a boil and dissolve the gelatin in it.
3. Place in refrigerator until it begins to congeal.
4. Add rhubarb, pickles, and celery.
5. Spoon in well-oiled individual molds or a large mold. Refrigerate until set.
6. Serve on lettuce leaf with Whipped Cream Dressing.

Serves 6 to 8.

GREEN GARDEN SALAD

2 CUPS COARSELY CUT
ENDIVE
2 CUPS COARSELY CUT
LETTUCE
1 CUP COARSELY CUT
SPINACH
1 CUP GRATED RAW
CAULIFLOWER
½ TEASPOON SALT
¼ TEASPOON PEPPER
½ TEASPOON CELERY SEED
⅛ TEASPOON GARLIC SALT

1. Toss first four ingredients together lightly.
2. Mix seasonings and toss among greens and cauliflower.
3. Place in refrigerator to chill. Just before serving mix with following dressing:

¼ CUP OIL
1 TABLESPOON CIDER
VINEGAR
½ TEASPOON SUGAR
¼ TEASPOON PAPRIKA

Serves 4.

MARASCHINO SALAD

1 PACKAGE STRAWBERRY GELATIN

1¾ CUPS TANGERINE JUICE (USE FROZEN, MIX AS DIRECTED ON CAN)

¼ CUP MARASCHINO CHERRY JUICE (DRAINED FROM CHERRIES)

1 TEASPOON VINEGAR

1 CUP FINELY CUT CELERY

1 CUP RAISINS

½ CUP CHOPPED PECANS

¼ CUP MARASCHINO CHERRIES, CUT UP

1. Bring tangerine juice to a boil.
2. Dissolve gelatin in hot juice.
3. Add cherry juice and vinegar.
4. Place in refrigerator until somewhat congealed. Add celery, raisins, nuts, and cherries.
5. Spoon into well oiled molds and refrigerate until set.
6. Serve with Whipped Cream Dressing.

Serves 8. Excellent for Valentine heart salad.

SOHO SALAD

1½ CUPS FINELY SHREDDED CABBAGE
½ CUP GRATED CARROTS
1 CUP SHREDDED COCO-NUT
1 CUP CRUSHED PINE-APPLE
3 TABLESPOONS VINEGAR
2 TABLESPOONS WATER
1 TABLESPOON CORN-STARCH
½ CUP PINEAPPLE JUICE
1 EGG YOLK, BEATEN
¾ CUP MAYONNAISE
1½ CUPS WHIPPED CREAM
1 CUP CHOPPED PEANUTS

1. Drain pineapple. Save the juice.
2. Mix cabbage, carrots, pineapple, and coconut together.
3. Mix vinegar with water and stir into the above mixture. Chill.
4. Mix cornstarch with pineapple juice. Cook in double boiler until thickened. Add egg yolk. Cook for 2 minutes. Cool mixture.
5. With egg beater beat mayonnaise into cooled mixture. Then fold in whipped cream.

6. Mix the completed dressing with cabbage mixture. Chill.
7. Serve on lettuce leaf and sprinkle toasted chopped peanuts over the top.

Serves 8 to 10.

SOUTHERN COLE SLAW

4 CUPS GRATED CABBAGE
¼ TEASPOON SALT
4 TABLESPOONS SUGAR
2 TABLESPOONS VINEGAR
½ CUP SALAD DRESSING
1 TEASPOON CELERY SEED

1. Prepare ingredients. Mix all together.
2. Chill before serving.

Serves 4 to 6.

Delicious cole slaw. So good with fried fish.

TEA GARDEN SALAD

1 PACKAGE ORANGE
GELATIN
1 CUP HOT FRESHLY MADE
BLACK TEA
1 CUP JUICE DRAINED
FROM ORANGES AND
PINEAPPLE
1 11 OZ. CAN MANDARIN
ORANGE SECTIONS
1 9 OZ. CAN CRUSHED
PINEAPPLE
1 5 OZ. CAN WATER CHEST-
NUTS

DRESSING
1 CUP WHIPPED CREAM   *Pg 110*
DRESSING
GRATED RIND OF 1
ORANGE
PINCH OF MACE

1. Dissolve gelatin in hot tea.
2. Add cup of juice from Mandarin oranges and pineapple. (Add regular orange juice to fill cup if
needed.) Stir.
3. Place gelatin in refrigerator until it has thickened
considerably.

103

4. Drain and cut water chestnuts into small slices.
5. Add chestnuts, pineapple, and orange sections to gelatin.
6. Spoon mixture into well-oiled molds.
7. Refrigerate until set.
8. Mix Whipped Cream Dressing with orange rind and mace. Serve on top of salad.

Serves 8. Tantalizingly different.

ROSALEE SALAD

¼ CUP FINELY CUT GREEN
ONIONS, USE STEMS AS
WELL
4 CUPS LETTUCE OR
OTHER SALAD GREENS,
TORN INTO PIECES
2 MEDIUM SIZED TO-
MATOES
SALT AND PEPPER
½ CUP SALAD OIL
¼ CUP LEMON JUICE

1. Place onions in bottom of salad bowl.
2. Add lettuce and top with peeled tomatoes, cut in sections.
3. Place in refrigerator until serving time.
4. Sprinkle with salt and pepper.
5. Distribute the salad oil over the top, then the lemon juice.
6. Toss the salad together and serve.

Makes 6 dinner sized salads.

Sunflower, sesame, poppy, or caraway seeds may be added at time of serving to give salad more zest.

TOSSED SALAD, INDONESIA

2 CUPS LETTUCE,
COARSELY SHREDDED
2 TOMATOES, CUT IN
PIECES
¼ CUP DICED CUCUMBER
¼ CUP DICED CELERY
¼ CUP CHOPPED GREEN
ONION
¼ CUP DICED RADISHES
¼ CUP CHOPPED RAW
CARROT
1 TABLESPOON CHOPPED
PARSLEY
¼ CUP CHOPPED CABBAGE
¼ TEASPOON PEPPER
¼ TEASPOON GARLIC SALT
¼ TEASPOON SALT
1½ CUPS COLD BROWNED
BUTTER RICE (PAGE 70)

1. Combine and mix all ingredients except rice. Place in refrigerator until serving time.
2. Just before serving add rice and toss together.
3. Serve on lettuce leaf with French dressing.

Serves 6 to 8. The browned butter rice adds zest.

TROPIC ISLE SALAD

1 1 LB. 13 OZ. CAN
    APRICOTS
1 PACKAGE ORANGE
    GELATIN
3 BANANAS, SLICED
1 CUP CHOPPED PECANS

1. Drain apricots. Measure juice and add enough water to make 1¾ cups.
2. Press apricots through a sieve.
3. Heat juice to a boil. Dissolve gelatin in the hot liquid. Place in refrigerator until gelatin begins to congeal.
4. Add apricot purée, sliced bananas, and nuts to the thickening gelatin.
5. Pour into well-oiled 8 x 8 inch pan, 2 inches deep. Refrigerate until congealed.
6. Cut into squares. Serve in lettuce cups with Whipped Cream Dressing.

Serves 12. Individual molds may be used if perferred.

WINTER SALAD

2 PACKAGES LIME GELATIN
4 CUPS BOILING WATER
1 CAN FROZEN LIMEADE
2 CUPS RAW CRANBERRIES,
   CUT UP
2 CUPS DICED CELERY
1 CUP DICED GREEN
   PEPPER

1. Dissolve gelatin in boiling water. Add frozen limeade and stir until dissolved.
2. Refrigerate to thicken until syrupy.
3. Cut each berry into 3 pieces. (Tedious, but can be
   done.)
4. When gelatin has thickened stir in berries, celery,
   and green pepper.
5. Spoon into well-oiled individual molds or one
   large mold.
6. Refrigerate until set.
7. Serve with Whipped Cream Dressing.

Makes 12 individual molds using ½ cup per mold.

A piquant salad to serve with a meat course.

VEGETABLES IN ASPIC JELLY

1 1/3 TABLESPOONS PLAIN
GELATIN
2/3 CUP COLD CHICKEN
BROTH
2 CUPS TOMATO JUICE
¼ CUP LEMON JUICE
2/3 TEASPOON SALT
⅛ TEASPOON PEPPER
2 TABLESPOONS SUGAR
2/3 CUP CUT, COOKED
GREEN BEANS
2/3 CUP GRATED RAW
CAULIFLOWER
1/3 CUP CHOPPED GREEN
PEPPER
¼ CUP FINELY CUT
GREEN ONIONS
2/3 CUP GRATED CABBAGE
¼ CUP CUT CUCUMBER
2/3 CUP CUT PECANS

1. Sprinkle gelatin over chicken broth. Let stand
10 minutes.
2. Heat tomato juice to a boil. Add to chicken broth.
Stir to dissolve gelatin.
3. Add salt, pepper, sugar, and lemon juice. Mix.
4. Refrigerate until gelatin begins to congeal. Add

109

cut vegetables and nuts. Mix. Spoon into oiled molds or pan. Refrigerate until set.

5. Serve with Whipped Cream Dressing.

Serves 12.

WHIPPED CREAM DRESSING

2 CUPS STIFFLY
WHIPPED CREAM
1 CUP MAYONNAISE

1. Fold mayonnaise into whipped cream.

ROQUEFORT-OLIVE DRESSING

½ CUP ROQUEFORT CHEESE
(BROKEN IN SMALL
PIECES)
½ CUP CHOPPED STUFFED
OLIVES
2 CUPS FRENCH DRESSING

1. Mix all ingredients together.
2. Chill. Serve over head lettuce or any green salad.

Serves 12.

FRENCH DRESSING No. 1

¾ CUP OIL
1/3 CUP VINEGAR
1 EGG YOLK
¼ TEASPOON SALT
¼ TEASPOON PEPPER
¼ TEASPOON PAPRIKA

1. Combine all ingredients and beat with egg beater until well blended.

FRENCH DRESSING No. 2

¼ CUP VINEGAR
½ CUP SALAD OIL
½ CUP TOMATO SOUP
1 TEASPOON WORCESTER-
SHIRE SAUCE
¼ TEASPOON SALT
⅛ TEASPOON PEPPER
2 TEASPOONS SUGAR
⅛ TEASPOON GARLIC SALT

1. Mix all ingredients in a blender or with an egg beater until well mixed.
2. Chill and serve with salads.

Serves 8.

CHICKEN SANDWICH TORGOR

TOAST
OLIVE BUTTER OR CHOPPED
STUFFED OLIVES
SLICED CHICKEN
BACON
SPICED CRAB APPLES

1. Spread 1 slice of toast with olive butter or chopped stuffed olives then sprinkle with finely chopped cooked bacon.
2. Arrange sliced chicken on top of the above mixture. Spread a small amount of mayonnaise over chicken. Top with another piece of buttered toast.
3. Cut sandwich in triangles and serve with a spiced crab apple.

CONTINENTAL SANDWICH

¼ CUP CHOPPED RAW
   SPINACH OR CHOPPED
   CELERY LEAVES
¼ CUP CHOPPED STUFFED
   OLIVES
¼ CUP CHOPPED NUTS
¼ CUP CHOPPED CAPERS

¼ CUP CHOPPED BAKED
   HAM
¼ CUP CHOPPED COOKED
   MUSHROOMS
¼ CUP CHOPPED HARD-
   COOKED EGG
2 TABLESPOONS MAYON-
   NAISE
SALT AND PEPPER
BREAD
LETTUCE
ITALIAN TOMATO

1. Mix first seven ingredients.
2. Add mayonnaise and season to taste. Mix to form a spread.
3. Toast bread on one side only. Butter untoasted side and spread with sandwich filling.
4. Top with buttered untoasted side next to filling.
5. Place lettuce leaf on top of sandwich with an Italian tomato.

Makes 6 sandwiches.

ASSORTED FINGER SANDWICHES

8 SLICES BOSTON BROWN
  BREAD
½ CUP ORANGE MARMA-
  LADE

*

2 SLICES WHITE BREAD
½ CUP FINELY CHOPPED
  COOKED SHRIMP
½ BAR CREAM CHEESE
  SALT AND PEPPER
1 TABLESPOON MAYON-
  NAISE

*

2 SLICES RYE BREAD
4 SLICES COOKED TONGUE

*

1 SLICE WHITE BREAD
1 SLICE WHOLE-WHEAT
  BREAD
½ CUP CHOPPED HARD-
  COOKED EGG
1 TEASPOON ANCHOVY
  PASTE
1 TABLESPOON MAYON-
  NAISE

2 SLICES WHOLE-WHEAT
BREAD
½ CUP GRATED RAW CAR-
ROT
½ CUP CHOPPED LETTUCE
SALT AND PEPPER
1 TABLESPOON MAYON-
NAISE
FEW DROPS LEMON
JUICE

1. Butter Boston brown bread and put together with orange marmalade.
2. Mix shrimp with cream cheese and mayonnaise, and season to taste. Spread between white bread and cut into 4 triangles by cutting from corner to corner.
3. Butter rye bread and place tongue on each slice of bread. Do not put this sandwich together. Cut each piece of bread in half.
4. Mix eggs, anchovy paste, and mayonnaise together. Spread between 1 slice of white and 1 slice of whole-wheat bread. Cut in 4 triangles.
5. Mix carrots, lettuce, mayonnaise, seasoning, and lemon juice. Spread between whole-wheat bread and cut into four finger pieces.
6. Place 1 marmalade, 1 shrimp, 1 tongue, 1 egg, and 1 carrot sandwich on each plate. In the center place a lettuce leaf filled with chopped salad.

Serves 4.

NOTES

NOTES

NOTES

BREADS

APPLE FRITTERS

1½ CUPS SIFTED FLOUR
2 TEASPOONS BAKING POWDER
¼ TEASPOON SALT
1 TABLESPOON SUGAR
1 TABLESPOON OLEOMAR-GARINE
1 EGG, BEATEN
½ CUP MILK
1 CUP DICED TART APPLES
1½ TEASPOONS LEMON EX-TRACT

1. Sift flour, salt, and baking powder together.
2. Cream sugar and oleomargarine. Add egg. Mix.
3. Add flour alternately with milk. Begin and end with some of the flour.
4. Add diced apples and extract. Mix.
5. Drop batter, about the size of a walnut, into deep fat at 300°-325° F. Fry until brown. About 4 minutes.
6. Remove from grease and drain well on a paper towel. Toss fritters in a mixture of 1 cup granulated sugar, ½ teaspoon nutmeg, and 1 teaspoon cinnamon.

Serve warm as a hot bread at lunch or for tea.

Makes 3 dozen fritters.

BANANA-CURRANT BREAD

½ CUP CURRANTS
1 CUP BOILING WATER
¾ CUP SUGAR
¼ CUP OLEOMARGARINE
2 EGGS, BEATEN
2 CUPS SIFTED FLOUR
2 TEASPOONS BAKING POWDER
½ TEASPOON SALT
1½ CUPS DICED BANANAS
1 TEASPOON ALMOND EXTRACT

1. Soak currants in boiling water for 5 minutes. Drain.
2. Blend sugar and oleomargarine. Add eggs. Mix well.
3. Sift flour, baking powder, and salt together. Add and mix well.
4. Add currants and mix.
5. Add bananas and extract. Mix.
6. Bake in well-greased loaf pan 13 x 4½ x 2½ at 350° F. for 1 hour.
7. Turn pan on side to cool.
8. Remove from pan and place in plastic bag or wrap in aluminum foil overnight. Cut in thin slices the next day.

An ideal moist bread for tea or lunch.

BUTTERMILK PILLOW ROLLS

1 CAKE COMPRESSED
YEAST
¼ CUP WARM WATER
⅛ CUP MELTED BUTTER
⅛ CUP MELTED LARD
¼ TEASPOON BAKING
SODA
1 CUP BUTTERMILK
4½ CUPS SIFTED FLOUR
2 EGGS
¼ CUP SUGAR
2 TEASPOONS SALT
1½ TABLESPOONS HONEY
MIXED WITH 1½ TABLE-
SPOONS MELTED
BUTTER

1. Dissolve yeast in warm water.
2. Add butter and lard. Mix.
3. Mix soda with buttermilk.
4. Add buttermilk mixture, with 1 cup flour, to yeast mixture. Mix well.
5. Add eggs, sugar, and salt. Mix.
6. Add the remaining flour. Beat well.
7. Knead mixture in bowl to blend together.
8. Place in a well-greased bowl. Cover and set in a warm place to rise until doubled in bulk.
9. Punch dough down and allow to rise about 1 hour.

10. Place dough on floured board, using about 2 tablespoons of flour on board. Pat or roll out to ½ inch thick and cut into 1½ inch squares.
11. Place squares on a greased baking sheet or pan. Brush tops with honey and melted butter mixture.
12. Allow rolls to rise once more. Bake at 375° F. for 12 minutes.

Makes 4 dozen pillows.

CINNAMON TWISTERS

¼ CUP OLEOMARGARINE
1 CUP SCALDED MILK
¼ CUP SUGAR
1 TEASPOON SALT
2 CAKES COMPRESSED YEAST
2 EGGS, BEATEN
4½ CUPS SIFTED FLOUR

SPREAD

¼ CUP MELTED OLEO-MARGARINE
¼ CUP HONEY
¾ CUP BROWN SUGAR
¾ CUP WHITE SUGAR
1½ TABLESPOONS FLOUR
1½ TEASPOONS CINNAMON

123

1. Dissolve oleomargarine in scalded milk.
2. Add sugar and salt. Stir.
3. When cooled to tepid temperature crumble in yeast. Stir to dissolve.
4. Add eggs and flour. Stir vigorously.
5. Place in a well-greased bowl and cover. Set in a warm place to rise until double in bulk.
6. Punch down dough and allow to rise again.
7. Place dough on lightly floured board and roll to ¼ inch thickness. Spread with melted oleomargarine and then the honey.
8. Mix sugars, flour, and cinnamon and sprinkle over the honey.
9. Cut dough into ½ inch wide strips. Braid 3 strips together and cut braids into 3½-inch long Twists. Pinch ends together.
10. Place in well-greased pan, ½ inch apart. Allow to rise until double in bulk.
11. Bake at 400° F. for 12 minutes. Remove from pan while hot.

Makes about 5 dozen Twisters.

CINNAMON KITES

4 BAKED CLOVER-LEAF
ROLLS
1 EGG, BEATEN
3 TABLESPOONS RICH MILK
½ CUP SUGAR MIXED WITH
½ TEASPOON CINNAMON
DEEP FAT FOR FRYING
PURPOSES

1. Separate rolls into sections.
2. Mix egg and milk.
3. Dip each section of roll into the egg wash.
4. Fry in deep fat, as for frying doughnuts, until brown.
5. Remove and drain on a paper towel to remove excess fat.
6. Toss each Kite in cinnamon sugar and serve hot.

Makes 12 Kites.

These Cinnamon Kites are much relished by guests at Boone Tavern Hotel.

CORN BREAD

2 CUPS WHITE CORN MEAL
½ CUP FLOUR
½ TEASPOON SALT
1 TEASPOON BAKING POWDER
½ TEASPOON BAKING SODA
2 CUPS BUTTERMILK
2 EGGS, WELL BEATEN
4 TABLESPOONS MELTED LARD

1. Sift corn meal, flour, salt, and baking powder together.
2. Mix soda with buttermilk. Add to dry ingredients. Beat well.
3. Add eggs and beat.
4. Add lard. Mix well.
5. Pour into well-greased, smoking hot, large skillet on top of stove.
6. Place on lower shelf of oven at 450° to 500° F. for 18 minutes. Move to upper shelf and bake 5 to 10 minutes longer.

It is important to heat well-greased skillet to smoking hot on top of stove before pouring in batter.

CURRY PUFFS

> **2 CUPS CORN BREAD, FINELY CRUMBLED**
> **⅛ TEASPOON PEPPER**
> **¼ TEASPOON SALT**
> **¼ TEASPOON CURRY POWDER**
> **1½ TEASPOONS BAKING POWDER**
> **1/3 CUP FINELY MINCED ONION**
> **2 EGGS, WELL BEATEN**

1. Mix the first 6 ingredients together.
2. Add eggs. Mix.
3. Shape into small balls size of a walnut. Place in refrigerator for 20 minutes.
4. Fry in deep fat until browned. Drain on paper towel.
5. Place puffs in the following sauce:

> **½ CUP CHICKEN FAT**
> **¼ CUP FLOUR**
> **1½ CUP RICH CHICKEN STOCK**
> **½ TEASPOON CURRY POWDER**
> **SALT AND PEPPER TO TASTE**

a) Melt chicken fat in top of double boiler.
b) Stir in flour and cook 3 minutes.
c) Add chicken stock. Stir frequently while cooking for 20 minutes.
d) Stir in curry powder, salt, and pepper.
e) Heat puffs in sauce for 30 minutes.

6. Serve the puffs in the curry sauce.

The Curry Puffs served in the sauce, similar to small dumplings served in gravy, are a popular meat accompaniment at Boone Tavern Hotel.

HONEY AND WALNUT COFFEE LOAF

2 CUPS SCALDED MILK
½ CUP SUGAR
¾ CUP OLEOMARGARINE
¾ TEASPOON SALT
1 CAKE COMPRESSED YEAST
7 CUPS SIFTED FLOUR
GRATED RIND OF 1 LEMON
GRATED RIND OF 1 ORANGE
2 EGGS, BEATEN
1 TEASPOON VANILLA

1. Add sugar, oleomargarine, and salt to scalded milk. Stir until dissolved.
2. When cooled to tepid temperature crumble in yeast. Stir until dissolved.
3. Add 2 cups flour, fruit rinds, egg, and vanilla. Beat well.
4. Add remaining flour. Mix well.
5. Place in a greased bowl and lightly grease top of dough. Cover and set in a warm place to rise until doubled in bulk.
6. Prepare the following filling:

1 CUP HONEY
1½ CUPS FINELY CHOPPED
WALNUTS
¼ TEASPOON CINNAMON
⅛ TEASPOON MACE
1 TABLESPOON CREAM
2 TABLESPOONS OLEO-
MARGARINE
1 EGG WHITE
2 TABLESPOONS SUGAR

   a) Bring honey to a boil. Add chopped nuts, cinnamon, mace, cream, and oleomargarine. Stir and allow to cool until warm.

   b) Add sugar to stiffly beaten egg white. Beat well. Fold into the above mixture.

7. When dough has doubled in bulk, roll out on a heavily floured cloth to ⅛ inch thickness.

Spread ¼ cup of melted oleomargarine over dough, then spread honey mixture over it. Roll up as for jelly roll. Either pinch or cut roll in half and pinch ends.

8. Place in 2 well-greased long loaf bread pans. Allow to rise until doubled in bulk.
9. Bake at 325° F. for 1 hour.
10. Turn out on a towel to cool. Cut in ½ inch thick slices and serve.

The Honey and Walnut Loaf resembles the often found coffee roll of Central European cookery.

ENGLISH GOOSEBERRY BREAD

1 EGG, BEATEN
½ CUP SUGAR
2 TABLESPOONS MELTED
  BUTTER
1 CUP GOOSEBERRY JAM
2 CUPS SIFTED FLOUR
3 TEASPOONS BAKING
  POWDER
¼ TEASPOON BAKING SODA
½ TEASPOON SALT
½ CUP MILK

1. Mix egg and sugar.
2. Add melted butter. Mix well.
3. Add jam. Mix.
4. Sift flour, baking powder, baking soda, and salt together. Add to the creamed mixture, alternating with the milk. Mix well.
5. Bake in a well-greased bread pan 5½ x 9 inch at 350° F. for 1 hour.
6. Turn bread out on wire rack to cool. This bread cuts best when allowed to stand for 12 hours.

Makes 1 loaf.

MOUNTAIN WOMAN COUNTRY CORNCAKES

1 CUP WHITE CORN MEAL
2 TABLESPOONS FLOUR
½ TEASPOON SALT
¼ TEASPOON BAKING SODA
1 CUP BUTTERMILK
1 EGG, BEATEN
2 TABLESPOONS MELTED
   LARD

1. Sift corn meal, flour, and salt together.
2. Mix soda with buttermilk. Add to above and mix.
3. Add egg and melted lard. Mix well.
4. Fry in a very hot iron skillet which has a light covering of lard. Turn as for pancakes to cook on both sides.

Makes 10 to 15 cakes—mighty good.

POPPY SEED AND CARAWAY ROLLS

1 CUP SCALDED MILK
¼ CUP OLEOMARGARINE
2 CAKES COMPRESSED
   YEAST

¼ CUP SUGAR
2 TEASPOONS SALT
2 EGGS, BEATEN
4 CUPS SIFTED FLOUR
½ CUP SIFTED CORN MEAL
⅛ CUP POPPY SEEDS
¾ TEASPOON CARAWAY
SEEDS

1. Melt oleomargarine in scalded milk.
2. When milk is cooled to tepid temperature, crumble in yeast and stir to dissolve.
3. Add sugar, salt, and eggs. Mix.
4. Add flour and corn meal. Mix well.
5. Add poppy and caraway seeds. Mix well.
6. Place dough in well-greased bowl and cover. Set in warm place to rise until doubled in bulk.
7. Punch down dough and allow to rise a second time. About 1 hour.
8. Shape dough into 1 inch balls. Place 3 balls in each well-greased muffin tin cup. Allow to rise until doubled in size.
9. Bake at 400° F. for 12 minutes.

Makes about 2 dozen rolls.

OATMEAL ROLLS

2 CUPS SCALDED MILK
½ CUP BUTTER
½ CUP SUGAR
2 TEASPOONS SALT
2 CAKES COMPRESSED YEAST
4 EGGS, WELL BEATEN
3 CUPS QUICK OATMEAL
6 CUPS SIFTED FLOUR

1. Dissolve butter, sugar, and salt in scalded milk.
2. When cooled to tepid temperature crumble in yeast and stir to dissolve.
3. Add eggs. Mix.
4. Add oatmeal and flour. Mix well. This is a soft dough.
5. Place in a well-greased bowl. Cover and set in warm place to rise until doubled in bulk.
6. Punch down dough and allow to rise a second time.
7. Roll dough out on floured board to ¾ inch thickness. Cut in rounds. Place on greased baking sheet and cover with a towel. Allow to rise until doubled in bulk.
8. Bake at 400° F. for 12 minutes.

Makes 7 dozen tasty rolls.

PEANUT BUTTER MUFFINS

½ CUP BROWN SUGAR, PACKED
¼ CUP OLEOMARGARINE
½ CUP PEANUT BUTTER
2 EGGS
1 CUP SIFTED FLOUR
1 CUP SIFTED WHOLE-WHEAT FLOUR
3 TEASPOONS BAKING POWDER
¼ TEASPOON SALT
1¼ CUPS MILK

1. Blend sugar and oleomargarine.
2. Add peanut butter and mix until creamy.
3. Add eggs and beat until smooth and creamy.
4. Sift the flours, salt, and baking powder together and add alternately with the milk. Begin and end with the flour. Mix well.
5. Bake in well-greased muffin pans at 400° F. for 12 to 15 minutes.

Yields 1½ dozen large or 2 1/3 dozen small muffins.

PUMPKIN MUFFINS

½ CUP SUGAR
½ CUP OLEOMARGARINE
1 CUP COOKED OR
   CANNED PUMPKIN
1 TABLESPOON MOLASSES
1 EGG, BEATEN
2 CUPS SIFTED FLOUR
¼ TEASPOON CINNAMON
¼ TEASPOON CLOVES
¼ TEASPOON NUTMEG
¼ TEASPOON MACE
1 TEASPOON SALT
1 TEASPOON BAKING
   POWDER
¾ CUP BUTTERMILK
1 TEASPOON BAKING SODA
1 CUP RAISINS

1. Blend sugar and oleomargarine.
2. Add pumpkin, molasses, and egg. Mix well.
3. Sift flour with spices, salt, and baking powder.
4. Mix soda with buttermilk.
5. Mix raisins with ½ cup of the sifted flour and spices.
6. Add remaining flour alternately with the buttermilk to the creamed mixture. Beat well.
7. Add raisins. Mix.

8. Place in well-greased small muffin tins.
9. Bake at 375° F. for 20 minutes. If large muffin tins are used bake for 25 minutes.

Makes 4 dozen very small muffins or 2 dozen large.

SPICE ROLLS

¼ CUP OLEOMARGARINE
1 CUP SCALDED ORANGE JUICE
¼ CUP SUGAR
1½ TEASPOONS SALT
2 CAKES COMPRESSED YEAST
2 EGGS, BEATEN
¼ CUP GRATED ORANGE RIND
5 CUPS SIFTED FLOUR
1 TEASPOON NUTMEG
1 TEASPOON MACE

1. Add oleomargarine to scalded orange juice.
2. When cooled to tepid temperature add sugar, salt, and crumble in yeast. Stir to dissolve.
3. Add eggs and orange rind. Mix.
4. Sift flour with nutmeg and mace. Add half to the

137

above. Beat well. Add remaining flour and mix well.

5. Place in a well-greased bowl. Lightly grease top of dough. Cover and set in warm place. Allow to rise until doubled in bulk.
6. Punch down dough and allow to rise again.
7. Roll out dough on floured board to ½ inch thickness. Cut in rounds (2 inch diameter). Place in well-greased baking pan.
8. Brush tops of rolls with ¼ cup melted oleomargarine and sprinkle generously with a mixture of ¼ teaspoon cinnamon and ½ cup sugar.
9. Allow rolls to rise until doubled in bulk.
10. Bake at 375° F. for 12 minutes.

Makes 5 dozen rolls.

STRAWBERRY BISCUITS

2 CUPS SIFTED FLOUR
¾ TEASPOON SALT
1 TABLESPOON BAKING POWDER
¼ CUP LARD
¼ TEASPOON BAKING SODA
1 CUP BUTTERMILK
½ CUP MELTED LARD
24 SMALL CUBES OF SUGAR
24 FRESH STRAWBERRIES

1. Sift flour with salt and baking powder.
2. Work in lard with fingertips.
3. Mix baking soda with buttermilk. Add to flour mixture, blending lightly.
4. Toss on a heavily floured pastry board and knead until soft and spongy.
5. Roll lightly to ½ inch thickness and cut into rounds.
6. Place in well-greased pan and brush tops with melted lard.
7. Press a small cube of sugar and a strawberry, side by side, into the center of each biscuit.
8. Allow biscuits to rise for 15 minutes.
9. Bake at 450° to 500° F. for 15 minutes.

Makes 2 dozen biscuits.

VARIATIONS FOR STRAWBERRY BISCUITS:

a) Chop 6 slices of crisp bacon and mix with dough before kneading.
b) Blackberries, blueberries, or a date may be used in place of the strawberry.

NUT BREAD

⅛ CUP OLEOMARGARINE
½ CUP SUGAR
2 EGGS, BEATEN
2 CUPS SIFTED FLOUR
2 TEASPOONS BAKING
  POWDER
1 TEASPOON SALT
¾ CUP MILK
¾ CUP CUT PECANS

1. Cream oleomargarine and sugar.
2. Add eggs. Mix.
3. Sift flour, baking powder, and salt together. Add alternately to the above mixture with milk. Begin and end with flour. Mix well.
4. Add pecans. Mix.
5. Place batter in a well-greased loaf pan 9 x 5½ inches. Bake at 350° F. for 50 minutes.
6. Turn loaf out on wire rack or towel to cool.

1 loaf of good nut bread. Will slice better if one day old.

SWEET ROLLS A LA DENMARK

1 CUP MILK
¼ CUP OLEOMARGARINE
¼ CUP SUGAR
1 TEASPOON SALT
1 CAKE COMPRESSED
    YEAST
2 EGGS, BEATEN
4½ CUPS SIFTED FLOUR

1. Scald milk and oleomargarine. Stir until dissolved.
2. Add sugar and salt. Stir well. Allow to cool until tepid.
3. Crumble yeast into liquid. Stir until dissolved.
4. Add eggs. Mix well.
5. Add 2 cups flour. Beat well. Add remaining flour and mix well.
6. Place in a well-greased bowl and lightly grease top of dough. Cover and set in warm place to rise until doubled in bulk.
7. Prepare filling:

½ CUP OLEOMARGARINE
1 CUP SUGAR
1½ TEASPOONS CINNAMON
¾ CUP ORANGE MAR-
    MALADE

141

a) Melt oleomargarine.

b) Mix sugar with cinnamon.

8. Remove dough to floured board and roll to ¼ inch thickness in a rectangular shape.

9. Spread dough with melted oleomargarine. Sprinkle with sugar and cinnamon mixture.

10. Roll up dough like a jelly roll. Cut into ½ or ¾ inch thick slices. Place on well-greased baking sheet.

11. On center of each roll place ½ teaspoon of Orange Marmalade or other jam or jelly.

12. Allow rolls to rise. Bake at 400° F. for 15 minutes.

13. Cool rolls and prepare the following icing:

> **1¼ CUPS CONFECTIONERS'
> SUGAR
> 2 TABLESPOONS MELTED
> OLEOMARGARINE
> 2 TABLESPOONS MILK
> ¼ CUP CHOPPED NUTS**

a) Mix confectioners' sugar with melted oleomargarine and milk. Beat well.

14. Spread icing over tops of rolls and sprinkle with chopped nuts.

Makes 40 rolls.

These are best when served heated.

WHOLE-WHEAT DINNER ROLLS

⅛ CUP SUGAR
2 TEASPOONS SALT
⅛ CUP MELTED LARD
1 CUP SCALDED MILK
1 COMPRESSED YEAST
CAKE
3 EGGS, BEATEN
1 CUP MASHED POTATOES
2 CUPS WHOLE-WHEAT
FLOUR
3 CUPS SIFTED WHITE
FLOUR

1. Add sugar, salt, and lard to the scalded milk.
2. When cooled to tepid temperature crumble in yeast and stir to dissolve.
3. Add eggs and mashed potatoes. Mix.
4. Add flours. Beat well. This is a soft dough.
5. Place in well-greased bowl and grease top of dough. Cover and set in warm place to rise until doubled in bulk.
6. Shape into 1 inch balls. Place 3 balls in each well-greased muffin tin cup.
7. Allow rolls to rise until doubled in size.
8. Bake at 400° F. for 12 minutes.

Makes 2½ dozen rolls.

NOTES

NOTES

"But the ample charms of a genuine Dutch country tea-table. . . . Such heaped-up platters of cakes of various and almost indescribable kinds. . . . There was the doughty dough-nut, the tenderer oly-koek, and the crisp and crumbling cruller; sweet cakes and short-cakes, ginger-cakes, and honey-cakes."

The Legend of Sleepy Hollow
Washington Irving

COOKIES AND PUNCH

DOATES

¾ CUP OLEOMARGARINE
1 CUP SIFTED FLOUR
2 CUPS CONFECTIONERS'
SUGAR
1 CUP QUICK OATMEAL
2 EGGS, BEATEN
¾ CUP CHOPPED PECANS
1 TEASPOON VANILLA

1. Blend oleomargarine, flour, oatmeal, and sugar by rubbing together with finger tips until crumbly.
2. Add eggs. Mix.
3. Add nuts and vanilla. Mix well.
4. Drop by teaspoonful onto a very well-greased tin, about 2 inches apart.
5. Bake at 300° F. for 20 minutes.
6. Run a spatula under each cookie to loosen from pan. Cool before removing from pan.

Makes 5 dozen Doates.

DRESDEN SLICES

½ CUP OLEOMARGARINE
1 CUP SUGAR
2 EGGS BEATEN
½ TEASPOON VANILLA
1 CUP SIFTED CAKE
FLOUR
¼ TEASPOON SALT
½ TEASPOON BAKING
SODA
5 TABLESPOONS BUTTER-
MILK
½ CUP LIQUID COFFEE
2½ SQUARES CHOCOLATE

1. Cream oleomargarine and sugar.
2. Add eggs and vanilla. Mix.
3. Sift flour and salt together. Mix soda with butter-milk and add alternately with flour to the above mixture. Mix well.
4. Heat coffee and melt chocolate in it. Stir until smooth and add to the above mixture. Blend well.
5. Spread batter into 3 well-greased 7½ x 11 inch pans.
6. Bake at 375° F. for 15 minutes.
7. Cool cakes and remove from pans one at a time, spreading frosting over each layer before topping with another layer.

FROSTING FOR
DRESDEN SLICES

6 CUPS SIFTED CONFEC-
TIONERS' SUGAR
2 TABLESPOONS CREAM
¼ CUP COCOA MIXED WITH
¼ CUP HOT COFFEE
1 TEASPOON VANILLA
2 TABLESPOONS MELTED
OLEOMARGARINE
1 CUP CHOPPED PECANS

a) Mix all ingredients except the nuts together and beat until fluffy.
b) Mix in the nuts. Spread the icing.
8. Cut cake in 1 x 3 inch slices.

This is a rich chocolate cake. Cuts best when one day old.

Makes about 24 slices.

FRUIT DROPS

½ CUP SUGAR
¼ CUP OLEOMARGARINE
2 EGGS, BEATEN
½ CUP APPLE SAUCE
1¼ CUPS SIFTED FLOUR
¼ TEASPOON SALT
½ TEASPOON CINNAMON
1 TEASPOON BAKING POWDER
½ CUP BUTTERMILK
½ TEASPOON BAKING SODA
1 CUP MIXED CANDIED FRUIT, DICED
½ CUP CHOPPED NUTS

1. Cream sugar and oleomargarine.
2. Add eggs and apple sauce. Mix.
3. Sift flour with salt, cinnamon, and baking powder.
4. Mix soda with buttermilk.
5. Add flour and buttermilk alternately to creamed mixture. Begin and end with some of the flour. Mix well.
6. Add fruit and nuts. Stir well.
7. Drop about 1½ teaspoonfuls into well-greased small muffin tins (1½ to 1¾ inch diameter muffin cup).

151

8. Bake at 350° F. for 13 to 15 minutes.
9. Cool for 10 minutes. Remove from pan and frost with the following icing:

> 2 CUPS SIFTED CONFEC-
> TIONERS' SUGAR
> 2 TABLESPOONS APPLE
> SAUCE
> 2 TABLESPOONS MELTED
> BUTTER

a) Mix all ingredients together and beat to a creamy consistency.
b) Frost tops of Fruit Drops.

Makes 2 dozen tiny Fruit Drops.
Try these for your cookie tray.

JUBILEE DOUGHNUTS

> 1 CUP SUGAR
> 1 TEASPOON NUTMEG
> 1 TEASPOON SALT
> 2 EGGS, WELL BEATEN
> 4 TABLESPOONS MELTED
> BUTTER
> 4 CUPS SIFTED FLOUR
> 5 TEASPOONS BAKING
> POWDER

1 CUP MILK
1 CUP CHOPPED PECANS
1 CUP DICED CANDIED
     FRUIT

1. Mix sugar, nutmeg, and salt.
2. Add eggs. Mix.
3. Add butter. Beat well.
4. Sift flour with baking powder. Mix 1 cup of flour with fruit and nuts.
5. Add remaining flour alternately with milk to egg mixture.
6. Add fruit and nut mixture. Mix well.
7. Roll dough on floured board to ¼ inch thickness. Cut with doughnut cutter and fry in deep fat at 350° to 370° F. Brown on one side then turn to brown other side. Drain on paper towel.
8. Roll hot doughnuts in sugar mixture made of 1 cup brown sugar and 1 cup white sugar.

Makes 4 dozen doughnuts.

Suggest serving with Hot Ruby Punch (page 171) for an evening snack.

MIDNIGHTS

3 SQUARES SEMISWEET
CHOCOLATE
¼ CUP OLEOMARGARINE
1 EGG, BEATEN WELL
1 TEASPOON VANILLA
3 OUNCE PACKAGE CREAM
CHEESE
¾ CUP FINE GRAHAM
CRACKER CRUMBS
1 TEASPOON BAKING
POWDER

1. Melt chocolate with oleomargarine over low heat.
2. Mix egg and vanilla.
3. Add cream cheese to egg mixture and beat well with beater.
4. Mix cracker crumbs with baking powder and add to the above.
5. Add chocolate, beating well as you make addition.
6. Drop by teaspoonful onto a well-greased tin. About 2 inches apart.
7. Bake at 325° F. for 15 minutes.

Makes 28 Midnights.

LITTLE PLUM CAKES

1 CUP OLEOMARGARINE
1½ CUPS BROWN SUGAR, PACKED
2 CUPS RAISINS, CUT UP
1½ CUPS CURRANTS
2 CUPS NUTS, CUT UP
2 CUPS DATES, CUT UP
2 CUPS MIXED CANDIED FRUIT
2 CUPS SIFTED FLOUR
1 TEASPOON BAKING SODA
3 TEASPOONS CINNAMON
½ TEASPOON NUTMEG
½ TEASPOON CLOVES
4 EGGS, BEATEN
1 CUP MILK
2 TEASPOONS VANILLA
½ CUP MOLASSES
½ CUP DARK KARO SYRUP
1 CUP JUICE FROM CANNED SPICED PEACHES

1. Cream oleomargarine and sugar.
2. Mix in raisins, currants, nuts, dates, and candied fruit.

3. Sift flour with soda, cinnamon, nutmeg, and cloves.
4. Mix eggs, milk, vanilla, molasses, syrup, and spiced peach juice together.
5. Add flour mixture alternately with liquid mixture to the fruit mixture. Mix well.
6. Spread in two greased 9 x 12 inch pans about ¾ inch deep.
7. Bake at 325° F. for 1 hour 15 minutes.
8. Cool. Cut into small squares and roll in granulated sugar. Keep in an air tight tin.

Makes about 85 little Plum Cakes.

MOMENTS OF BLISS

1 CUP BOILING WATER
¼ CUP BUTTER
1 CUP SIFTED FLOUR
4 EGGS
½ CUP SUGAR
1 CUP CHOPPED PECANS
1 TEASPOON MAPLE EX-
TRACT

1. Bring water to a rolling boil. Add butter and stir to dissolve.
2. Add flour all at once. Stir vigorously to prevent batter from sticking and burning to pan.
3. Cook mixture until it forms a ball in center of pan. Allow to cool slightly.
4. Add eggs, one at a time. Beat well after each addition. An electric beater is helpful for this part of the work.
5. Beat in sugar, nuts, and extract.
6. Drop by half teaspoonful into deep fat at 300° F. Fry until nicely brown. About 2 or 3 minutes.
7. Drain on paper towel and toss in confectioners' sugar.

Makes 60 to 70 Moments of Bliss.

PLANTATION GINGERBREAD

¼ CUP SUGAR
¼ CUP OLEOMARGARINE
1 EGG, WELL BEATEN
1¼ CUPS SIFTED FLOUR
¼ CUP COOKED OR
CANNED PUMPKIN
½ CUP NEW ORLEANS
MOLASSES
1 TEASPOON BAKING
SODA
½ TEASPOON CLOVES
½ TEASPOON CINNAMON
½ TEASPOON GINGER
6 TABLESPOONS WATER

1. Cream sugar and oleomargarine.
2. Add egg with 1 cup flour. Beat well.
3. Add pumpkin and molasses. Beat well.
4. Sift remaining flour with soda and spices. Add with water to above mixture. Beat well.
5. Pour batter into a well-greased 9 x 13 x 2 inch pan.
6. Bake at 350° F. for 30 minutes.
7. When cake is cooled sift confectioners' sugar over top. Cut into ½ inch by 3 inches long pieces.

Makes 36 pieces.

A very good idea for the tea table.

OATMEAL DELIGHTS

1 CUP SUGAR
1 CUP OLEOMARGARINE
2½ CUPS SIFTED FLOUR
2½ CUPS QUICK OATMEAL
½ TEASPOON SALT
1 TEASPOON BAKING SODA
½ CUP HONEY
¼ CUP HOT WATER

1. Cream sugar and oleomargarine.
2. Mix flour, oatmeal, and salt together.
3. Mix soda with honey and hot water.
4. Add flour mixture alternately with liquid to creamed mixture. Begin and end with some of the flour. Mix well.
5. Place on a well-floured board. Flour rolling pin and roll to about ¼ inch thickness.
6. Cut in small rounds and place on greased cookie sheet.
7. Top center of each round with half teaspoonful of filling. Place another cookie round on top. Press edges together.
8. Bake at 375° F. for 12 to 15 minutes.

FILLING FOR
OATMEAL DELIGHTS

½ LB. RAISINS
1 WHOLE ORANGE
1 WHOLE LEMON
2 TABLESPOONS WATER
½ CUP SUGAR

1. Cut orange and lemon in quarters. Remove seeds and grind pulp and rind.
2. Add raisins, water, and sugar.
3. Cook on medium heat to thicken. Stir frequently.
4. Cool before placing on cookies.

Makes about 44 cookies.

YULE LOGS

2 TABLESPOONS GRATED
ORANGE PEEL
2 TABLESPOONS GRATED
LEMON PEEL
½ CUP CHOPPED PECANS
½ CUP GRATED COCONUT
½ CUP SIFTED FLOUR
¼ CUP OLEOMARGARINE
¼ CUP SUGAR
2 EGG YOLKS, BEATEN
2 EGG WHITES, STIFFLY
BEATEN

¼ TEASPOON BAKING SODA
¼ TEASPOON BAKING POWDER
¼ CUP APPLE CIDER

1. Mix the first 4 ingredients with ¼ cup flour.
2. Cream oleomargarine and sugar.
3. Add egg yolks to creamed mixture.
4. Sift the remaining flour with baking soda and baking powder.
5. Add to creamed mixture alternately with cider.
6. Add the fruit and nut mixture. Mix well.
7. Fold in egg whites.
8. Bake in well-greased 7 x 11 inch pan at 300° F. for 30 minutes.
9. Cool and cut in 1 x 2½ inch pieces. Roll in granulated sugar.

Makes about 40 Logs.

NUTKINS

1 EGG WHITE
1 CUP SIFTED CONFEC-
  TIONERS' SUGAR
1 CUP FINELY CHOPPED
  PECANS
½ TEASPOON VANILLA

1. Beat egg white until frothy and standing in peaks.
2. Fold in sugar and nuts. Add vanilla.
3. Drop by teaspoonful onto a well-greased cookie sheet.
4. Bake at 325° F. for 15 to 20 minutes.
5. Remove from oven and allow to set for 10 minutes before lifting from cookie sheet with spatula.

Makes 20 nutty cookies.

PRUNEAUX

1 CUP HOT PRUNE
   JUICE
1 CUP DRIED PRUNES,
   CUT IN SMALL PIECES
1 CUP SUGAR
2 TABLESPOONS BUTTER
1 EGG, SEPARATED
1 TEASPOON SODA
1 1/3 CUPS SIFTED FLOUR
½ CUP CHOPPED NUTS

1. Pour hot prune juice over prunes and allow to stand for 10 minutes.
2. Cream sugar and butter. Add beaten egg yolk. Mix.
3. Mix soda with the prunes and juice. Add alternately with flour to the creamed mixture. Begin and end with some flour.
4. Add nuts. Mix well.
5. Fold in stiffly beaten egg white.
6. Bake in a 9 x 12 inch pan at 325° F. for 40 minutes.
7. Allow to cool. Cut in small squares and coat all sides with sifted confectioners' sugar.

Makes 28 delicious cookies.

RAISIN GEMS

¾ CUP BROWN SUGAR,
PACKED
½ CUP OLEOMARGARINE
2 EGGS
1½ CUPS SIFTED CAKE
FLOUR
1 TEASPOON BAKING
POWDER
¼ TEASPOON SALT
1 CUP RAISINS

1. Cream sugar and oleomargarine.
2. Add eggs, one at a time, beating well after each addition.
3. Sift flour, baking powder, and salt together.
4. Add to the creamed mixture alternately with the raisins. Mix well with each addition of raisins.
5. Drop by teaspoonful onto a well-greased cookie sheet.
6. Bake at 350° F. for 12 minutes.
7. Run a spatula under cookies while still hot.

Makes 4½ dozen cookies.

Coconut is a good substitute for the raisins.

SPICE DROPS

½ CUP OLEOMARGARINE
½ CUP SUGAR
2 EGGS, BEATEN
2 CUPS SIFTED CAKE FLOUR
½ TEASPOON SALT
2 TEASPOONS BAKING POWDER
¼ TEASPOON MACE
¼ TEASPOON CLOVES
¼ TEASPOON NUTMEG
1 TABLESPOON MILK
½ TEASPOON VANILLA
1 CUP DATES, CUT IN PIECES

1. Cream oleomargarine and sugar.
2. Add eggs. Mix.
3. Sift flour, salt, baking powder, and spices together.
4. Add half the flour to creamed mixture with milk and vanilla. Beat well.
5. Add remaining flour and dates. Beat well.
6. Shape into balls the size of an English walnut and roll in granulated sugar.
7. Place on a very well-greased cookie sheet about 1½ inches apart.
8. Bake at 275° F. for 10 to 12 minutes. Then turn

on broiler to brown cookies slightly. About 3 minutes.

5 dozen cookies.

ZANZIBARS

½ CUP OLEOMARGARINE
½ CUP SUGAR
1 EGG, BEATEN
1 TEASPOON VANILLA
1 CUP SIFTED FLOUR
1/3 CUP SUGAR MIXED
    WITH 1 TEASPOON CINNAMON
1 CUP GRATED COCONUT

1. Cream oleomargarine and sugar.
2. Add egg and vanilla. Mix. Add flour. Mix.
3. Spread in well-greased 7 x 11 inch pan.
4. Sprinkle top with mixture of sugar, cinnamon, and coconut. Press slightly into dough.
5. Bake at 375° F. for 25 minutes.
6. Cut into 1 x 2¼ inch bars while warm.

Makes 36 bars.

TAFFY CRISPS

½ CUP BROWN SUGAR
¼ CUP OLEOMARGARINE
1 EGG, BEATEN
¼ CUP MOLASSES
1 CUP SIFTED FLOUR
¼ TEASPOON SALT
½ TEASPOON BAKING POWDER
½ TEASPOON BAKING SODA
1½ TEASPOONS HOT WATER
½ CUP DATES, CUT UP

1. Blend sugar and oleomargarine.
2. Add egg and molasses. Mix.
3. Sift flour with salt and baking powder.
4. Mix baking soda with hot water.
5. Add flour and soda to creamed mixture. Mix well.
6. Stir in dates.
7. Drop by teaspoonful onto a well-greased cookie sheet.
8. Bake 8 or 10 minutes at 350° F. Remove cookies from cookie sheet while warm.

Makes about 50.

FROSTY MINT CUP

30 FRESH MINT LEAVES,
CUT UP
1 CUP WATER
½ CUP SUGAR
2 CUPS LIMEADE (USE
FROZEN AND FOLLOW
DIRECTIONS ON CAN)
1½ QUARTS LIME SHERBET
16 SPRIGS OF MINT LEAVES
GRANULATED SUGAR

1. Boil cut leaves, sugar, and water for 10 minutes.
2. Strain and chill the liquid.
3. Add limeade. Mix.
4. Just before serving add sherbet. Mix with beater until frothy.
5. Pour into sherbet cups. Garnish with washed mint sprigs which have been tossed in granulated sugar.

Serves 16 to 18.

Variations: Use 1 pint of sherbet to 1 cup of any kind of fruit juice mixture and froth with a beater.

FRESH PEACH TORCELLO

3 MEDIUM-SIZE RIPE
PEACHES
2 TABLESPOONS SUGAR
1½ CUPS CHIPPED ICE
¼ CUP COLD WATER

1. Wash and quarter peaches. Do not peel.
2. Place in an electric blender.
3. Add sugar, water, and ice. Blend at high speed.

Serve immediately in chilled glasses.
Serves 4.

OREGON PUNCH

1 CUP PRUNE JUICE
1 CUP GRAPE JUICE
1 CUP ORANGE JUICE
1 CUP APPLE JUICE

1. Mix all juices together.
2. Chill and serve.

Serves 8 punch cups. Average punch cup holds ½ measuring cupful.

MONTREAUX GRAPE CUP

6 TABLESPOONS SUGAR
1½ CUPS WATER
3 WHOLE CARDAMON
SEEDS
STICK CINNAMON
BROKEN UP TO MAKE 1
TEASPOON
1 CUP GRAPE JUICE

1. Break open cardamon seeds. Take out tiny seeds and discard shells.
2. Boil sugar, water, cardamon seeds, and cinnamon stick for 10 minutes.
3. Strain. Add grape juice to strained liquid.
4. Chill and serve.

Serves 6.

QUINCE BLOSSOM PUNCH

2 CUPS GRAPEFRUIT JUICE
2 CUPS ORANGE JUICE
1 CUP MARSCHINO CHERRY
JUICE

1. Mix the 3 juices.
2. Chill and serve.

Serves 10 punch cups. Average punch cup holds ½ measuring cupful.

RUBY CUP

2 1 LB. CANS STRAINED
CRANBERRY SAUCE
1 QUART APPLE JUICE
JUICE OF 2 ORANGES
JUICE OF 1 LEMON

1. Mix all. Beat with wire whip to blend well.
2. Bring to a boil.
3. Serve hot. May also be served as a chilled punch.

Serves 12 to 14.

RASPBERRY SHRUB

1 10 OZ. PACKAGE FROZEN
RASPBERRIES
3 CUPS WATER
¼ CUP FRESH LIME JUICE
GRATED RIND OF 1 LIME
JUICE OF 1 LEMON
¼ CUP SUGAR
1 CUP TANGERINE JUICE
(PREPARED FROM FROZEN
TANGERINE JUICE AS
DIRECTED ON CAN)

1. Boil raspberries with 2 cups of the water for 5 minutes.
2. Strain boiled mixture, pressing the berries through sieve into the strained liquid.
3. Add remaining 1 cup water, lime juice, lime rind, lemon juice, sugar, and tangerine juice to strained raspberry liquid and pulp.
4. Mix well and chill.

Serves 8 punch cups. Average punch cup holds ½ measuring cupful.

RED CLOVER PUNCH

1 1 LB. CAN SOUR
CHERRIES
½ CUP SUGAR
8 WHOLE CLOVES
1 CUP WATER
1 CUP APPLE JUICE

1. Drain cherries and save the juice.
2. Mix cherries, sugar, cloves, and water. Boil 15 minutes.
3. Strain boiled mixture, pressing half of the cherry pulp through sieve into strained liquid. Discard remaining pulp.
4. Mix strained liquid and pulp with juice from drained cherries and apple juice.
5. A drop of red coloring to be added if needed. Chill well.

Serves 6 punch cups. Average punch cup holds ½ measuring cupful.

STRAWBERRY BLOOM PUNCH

1 10 OZ. BOX FROZEN
    STRAWBERRIES
1 PINT WATER
¼ CUP SUGAR
1 6 OZ. CAN FROZEN
    LEMONADE

1. Boil strawberries, water, and sugar for 5 minutes.
2. Strain and press berries through a sieve.
3. Mix lemonade as directed on can to make 1 quart.
4. Add 2½ cups of lemonade to strained juice and pulp.
5. Chill before serving.

   Serves 16.

TOM SAWYER PUNCH

1 NO. 300 CAN BLUEBER-
    RIES
1 CUP BLUEBERRY JUICE
    (DRAINED FROM BERRIES)
1 CUP WATER
½ CUP GRAPE JUICE
1 CUP GRAPEFRUIT JUICE

1. Drain berries. Save juice for Step 3.
2. Boil berries and water for 10 minutes. Strain and press through sieve.
3. Mix all juices with the strained blueberry mixture.
4. Chill and serve.

Serves 8.

DAFFODIL PUNCH

3 CUPS APRICOT NECTAR
2 CUPS PINEAPPLE JUICE
2 TEASPOONS VANILLA

1. Mix all ingredients together and chill.
2. Stir well before pouring into punch cups.

Serves 10 punch cups. (Average punch cup holds ½ measuring cupful.)

NOTES

NOTES

DESSERTS

ALSATIAN BLUE PLUMS

CRUST

> 1 CUP GRAHAM CRACKER CRUMBS
> ½ CUP SUGAR
> 3 TABLESPOONS MELTED OLEOMARGARINE
> ½ TEASPOON CINNAMON

1. Mix cracker crumbs, cinnamon, sugar, and melted oleomargarine.
2. Press into bottom and sides of a 8 x 9 inch baking pan.

FILLING

> 2 ONE POUND CANS PURPLE PLUMS IN SYRUP, CUT PLUMS INTO PIECES, SAVE JUICE
> ½ CUP WHITE SUGAR
> ½ CUP BROWN SUGAR
> 1 CUP BREAD CRUMBS, MADE FROM TOASTED BREAD
> 4 TABLESPOONS MELTED OLEOMARGARINE
> 1 TABLESPOON FLOUR
> 1 TEASPOON CINNAMON

3. Arrange cut plums over crumb crust. Pour juice over plums.
4. Mix sugars, bread crumbs, oleomargarine, cinnamon, and flour. Sprinkle over top of plums.
5. Bake at 350° F. for 35 minutes. Then turn on broiler to brown for a few minutes.
6. Serve with a dab of whipped cream.

Serves 10.

BUTTERSCOTCH TOPPING

¼ CUP WHITE SUGAR
¼ CUP BROWN SUGAR
½ CUP WATER
⅛ TEASPOON BAKING SODA
2 TABLESPOONS OLEOMARGARINE

1. Mix sugars and soda.
2. Add water and mix.
3. Bring to a boil and cook slowly for 10 minutes.
4. Add oleomargarine and stir until blended.

Serve hot or cold over ice cream.

Serves 6.

AMBER GLACÉ

½ CUP WHITE SUGAR
½ CUP BROWN SUGAR
½ CUP ORANGE JUICE
½ CUP CRUSHED PEANUT
BRITTLE
1 PINT VANILLA ICE
CREAM
WHIPPED CREAM

1. Mix the sugars and orange juice.
2. Bring to a boil. Turn heat to low and continue boiling for 10 minutes.
3. Cool mixture.
4. Place ice cream in sherbet dishes and top with the sauce.
5. Shower crushed peanut brittle over ice cream.
6. Top with whipped cream.

This recipe serves 4 to 6, depending on size of servings.

Note: The sauce delights in climbing out of the pan as it cooks. A low heat is needed in the boiling process.

This simple sauce makes a strikingly unusual dessert.

OLD ENGLISH HARD SAUCE

¼ IB. BUTTER
1½ CUPS SUPERFINE SUGAR
1 EGG
2 TABLESPOONS VANILLA

1. Beat butter until fluffy.
2. Add sugar. Beat well.
3. Add egg and vanilla.
4. Beat until a light whipped consistency.

A very nice method of serving hard sauce is to shape in form of a large rosette by using a pastry bag and large star tube. Shape each rosette onto wax paper and place in refrigerator to chill before serving.

The ideal sauce to serve with gooseberry pie, hot mincemeat pie, fruit cobblers, and steamed puddings.

Makes 30 rosettes.

BOYSENBERRY COBBLER

2½ CUPS BOYSENBERRIES
3 CUPS JUICE DRAINED
FROM BERRIES
6 TABLESPOONS CORN-
STARCH

1 CUP SUGAR
4 TABLESPOONS OLEO-
MARGARINE

1. Heat juice in double boiler.
2. Mix cornstarch and sugar. Add to juice and cook over medium heat until thickened. About 10 minutes. Stir frequently.
3. Add oleomargarine and the berries.
4. Line a 7 x 9 x 2 inch baking pan with pastry crust. Pour in berry mixture. Top with pastry crust and prick a few holes in crust with fork. Bake at 450° F. for 40 minutes.

Blackberries maybe substituted for Boysenberries.

Pastry Crust

2 CUPS SIFTED FLOUR
¼ TEASPOON SALT
¼ TEASPOON BAKING
POWDER
¾ CUP LARD
4 TABLESPOONS COLD
WATER

1. Mix flour, salt, and baking powder.
2. Add lard and work into flour mixture with fingers.

3. Add water and blend.
4. Divide dough in 2 parts and roll out on floured
   board to ⅛ inch thickness.

CHERRY COBBLER

2 1 LB. CANS SOUR CHER-
RIES
CHERRY JUICE DRAINED
FROM BERRIES AND
ENOUGH ORANGE JUICE
TO MAKE UP 2 CUPS OF
JUICE
6 TABLESPOONS CORN-
STARCH
1½ CUPS SUGAR
4 TABLESPOONS OLEO-
MARGARINE
½ TEASPOON ALMOND
EXTRACT

1. Follow method given with Boysenberry Cobbler.

Serves 8 to 10.

Guests like Cobbler a la Mode.

CHARLOTTE OF APRICOTS

2 DOZEN LADY FINGERS
2 PACKAGES ORANGE
GELATIN
2 CUPS HOT ORANGE
JUICE (FROZEN ORANGE
JUICE MAY BE USED)
1½ CUPS COOKED APRICOTS
1 PINT WHIPPED CREAM
GRATED RIND OF 1
ORANGE
1 CUP SHREDDED COCO-
NUT
½ CUP SUGAR
3 EGG WHITES

1. Dissolve gelatin in hot orange juice. Refrigerate until considerably thickened, but not congealed.
2. Use dried apricots, 2 cups, cook in just enough water to cover until soft.
3. When gelatin is about thickened, place the apricots, sugar, and egg whites in electric mixer and whip at high speed.
4. When this mixture is light and fluffy add gelatin and continue to whip.
5. Whip cream until stiff and fold into the mixture. Fold in orange rind and finely shredded coconut.
6. Oil a spring mold or use an angel food pan. Cover bottom with half of the lady fingers. Stand the

remaining fingers on ends around the sides of the pan.

7. Pour the mixture in and allow to refrigerate until set.
8. Top each serving with a dab of whipped cream which has been sweetened with confectioners' sugar (a cup of whipped cream with 3 tablespoons of sugar).

This type of dessert was popular many years ago and today wins admiration and praise.

CHOCOLATE ALMOND SAUCE

¼ CUP SUGAR
¼ CUP COLD COFFEE
1 TABLESPOON COCOA
½ TEASPOON VANILLA
¼ CUP TOASTED ALMONDS

1. Mix all ingredients except the almonds together.
2. Boil for 3 minutes.
3. Sliver almonds and add.
4. Serve hot or cold over ice cream.

Serves 4.

FRESH BLUEBERRY ROLL

6 EGGS, SEPARATED
1 CUP SUGAR
¾ TABLESPOON GRATED
   LEMON RIND
1 TABLESPOON LEMON
   JUICE
¼ TEASPOON SALT
½ TEASPOON VANILLA
1 CUP SIFTED CAKE FLOUR

1. Beat egg whites until stiff and add half the sugar by folding in with long strokes to incorporate as much air as possible into the mixture.
2. Beat egg yolks until lemon colored. Add remaining sugar, lemon rind, juice, salt, and vanilla. Beat very well.
3. Fold egg yolk mixture into egg whites. Fold in flour carefully.
4. Dust a 10 x 15 inch baking sheet with flour and spread batter.
5. Bake at 325° F. for 30 minutes.
6. Cool slightly. Turn out on a towel which has been dusted with confectioners' sugar.
7. Spread with the following filling:

3 CUPS FRESH OR FROZEN
   BLUEBERRIES
1½ CUPS SUGAR

3 TABLESPOONS CORN-
STARCH
½ CUP COLD WATER

a) Mix blueberries with sugar.
b) Mix cornstarch with cold water and add to berries.
c) Cook on medium heat for 15 minutes to thicken. Stir carefully to avoid burning and breaking berries.
d) Cool before spreading on cake.

8. Roll up as for a jelly roll.
9. Allow to set for ½ hour.
10. Cut into thin slices. Serve 2 or 3 slices per person garnished with sweetened whipped cream.

Serves 12.

JAVA VELVET

½ CUP SUGAR
¼ CUP WATER
1 TABLESPOON INSTANT COFFEE
2½ CUPS SCALDED MILK
3 EGGS, SLIGHTLY BEATEN
2 TABLESPOONS SUGAR
¼ TEASPOON SALT
1 TEASPOON VANILLA

1. Mix sugar, water, and coffee. Boil 6 minutes.
2. Divide the coffee mixture equally into 6 well-buttered custard cups.
3. Slowly add scalded milk to eggs, mixing as you add.
4. Add sugar, salt, and vanilla. Mix.
5. Strain and slowly fill custard cups.
6. Bake 1 hour at 325° F.
7. Cool for 15 minutes. Turn out into serving dishes. Serve with a dab of whipped cream.

A good way to dress up custard with a coffee flavor.

Serves 6.

LIME-RICE PUDDING

1 CUP QUICK COOKING
RICE
2 EGG YOLKS, BEATEN
½ CUP SUGAR
GRATED RIND OF 1 LIME
¼ CUP LIME JUICE
2 TABLESPOONS MELTED
OLEOMARGARINE
1 CUP HOT WATER

1. Mix egg yolks, juice, rind, water, and sugar. Stir in rice.
2. Stir in melted oleomargarine.
3. Pour into a casserole. Cover and bake at 350° F. for 40 minutes.•
4. Remove from oven and spoon the following meringue over the top:

2 STIFFLY BEATEN EGG
WHITES
6 TABLESPOONS SUGAR
½ TEASPOON VINEGAR

a) Gradually add sugar to egg whites, beating as you make this addition.
b) Beat in vinegar.
c) Spoon on pudding top.

5. Return to oven to bake for 15 minutes longer.

An old-fashioned pudding. It can be made with lemons if you prefer.

LONDONDERRY BETTY

2 CUPS APPLES, QUAR-
  TERED, PEELED
¼ CUP WATER
½ CUP SUGAR
4 CUPS BREAD CUBES
1 CUP SUGAR
1 TEASPOON CINNAMON
½ CUP MELTED OLEOMAR-
  GARINE
½ CUP CHOPPED PECANS
½ CUP STRAINED HONEY

1. Mix apples, water, and ½ cup sugar. Stew for 5 minutes.
2. Toast half of the bread cubes and mix with half the sugar and half of the cinnamon. Add half of the melted oleomargarine and mix.
3. Butter an 8 x 10 pan and place the toasted bread mixture over the bottom. Spread cooked apples over this mixture.
4. Mix the remaining untoasted bread cubes with the remaining sugar and cinnamon. Add the re-

maining melted oleomargarine and mix. Spread this mixture over the apples.

5. Sprinkle pecans over the top, then dribble the honey over the surface.
6. Bake at 400° F. for 20 to 30 minutes.
7. Serve warm with whipped cream or ice cream.

Makes 8 to 12 servings. Old-fashioned goodness.

PALM SPRINGS DELIGHT

1 TABLESPOON PLAIN GELATIN
3 CUPS MILK
½ CUP SUGAR
¼ TEASPOON SALT
3 EGG YOLKS, BEATEN
1 CUP DATES, CUT FINE
½ TEASPOON ALMOND EXTRACT
½ TEASPOON VANILLA
3 STIFFLY BEATEN EGG WHITES

TOPPING

1 CUP WHIPPED CREAM
½ CUP CHOCOLATE SHOT
1 TEASPOON VANILLA

1. Soak gelatin in milk 5 minutes.
2. Place milk and gelatin in double boiler. Heat and stir to dissolve gelatin.
3. Add sugar and salt. Stir well.
4. Add egg yolks. Stir and cook until slightly thickened.
5. Add dates. Beat well to break up dates. Add extracts. Mix.
6. Remove from fire and fold in stiffly beaten egg whites.
7. Place in well-oiled mold. Refrigerate until set.
8. Unmold and serve each portion with a dash of the whipped cream that has been mixed with vanilla and chocolate shot.

Serves 8.

PEARS PUNJAB

1 LEMON
1 ORANGE
1 1 LB. 13 OZ. CAN PEAR HALVES IN HEAVY SYRUP (7 PEARS)
½ CUP SUGAR
¼ CUP WHIPPING CREAM
1 PINT VANILLA ICE CREAM

3 SQUARES SWEET CHOCO-
LATE, GRATED

1. Grate lemon and orange rind. Extract juice from fruit.
2. Mix the juice from pears and the above with sugar. Boil 15 minutes.
3. Allow this liquid to cool slightly and pour over the pear halves. Cover and refrigerate for 10 hours.
4. Just before serving whip the cream.
5. Place a pear half in stemmed sherbet. Pour some liquid over the pear, then about ¼ cup of ice cream. Top with a generous teaspoon of whipped cream and sprinkle with 1 teaspoon of grated chocolate.

This dessert has all the charm of India with its tantalizing flavor.

Serves 7.

Suggest you make the sauce the night before or in the morning to serve at dinner.

NOTES

NOTES

NOTES

CAKES

APPALACHIAN DRIED APPLE CAKE

½ CUP DRIED APPLES, CUT
IN SMALL PIECES
½ CUP APPLE CIDER
½ CUP BUTTER
2 EGGS, BEATEN
1 CUP SUGAR
½ CUP BUTTERMILK
¾ TEASPOON BAKING SODA
2 CUPS SIFTED CAKE
FLOUR
½ TEASPOON SALT

1. Simmer apples and cider for 10 minutes.
2. Cream sugar and butter.
3. Add the beaten eggs.
4. Sift flour and salt together.
5. Mix soda with buttermilk.
6. Add flour and buttermilk alternately. Begin and end with the flour.
7. Add apples and beat well.
8. Bake in a well-greased 9 x 13 x 2 inch pan at 350° F. for 30-35 minutes.
9. Cool the cake and frost with the following icing:

½ CUP DRIED APPLES, CUT
IN SMALL PIECES
½ CUP APPLE CIDER

3½ CUPS CONFECTIONERS'
SUGAR
¼ CUP MELTED BUTTER

1. Simmer apples and cider together for 10 minutes.
2. Sift sugar and add melted butter. Blend.
3. Add apple mixture and beat together until creamy.
   Frost cake.

An "old-timey" cake with an "old-timey" flavor.
Keeps well due to the apple content retaining the
moisture.

BAHAMA CAKE

½ CUP SUGAR
½ CUP OLEOMARGARINE
4 EGG YOLKS
1¼ CUPS SIFTED CAKE
FLOUR
¼ TEASPOON SALT
1½ TEASPOONS BAKING
POWDER
5 TABLESPOONS MILK
½ CUP COCONUT
1 TEASPOON ALMOND EX-
TRACT
5 EGG WHITES
1 CUP SUGAR
1 CUP COCONUT

1. Cream sugar and oleomargarine.
2. Beat egg yolks until light and creamy. Add to the above.
3. Sift flour with baking powder and salt. Add alternately with milk. Mix well.
4. Add ½ cup coconut and almond extract. Mix.
5. Spread batter in 2 well-greased cake pans. This is a thin layer of batter.
6. Beat egg whites until stiff and frothy. Add 1 cup of sugar. Continue beating while adding sugar until the egg whites stand in peaks.
7. Spread meringue over the 2 cake batters.
8. Sprinkle 1 cup coconut on top of meringue.
9. Bake at 325° F. for 30 minutes. Cool on cake racks.
10. Prepare the following filling:

1 EGG YOLK
½ CUP SUGAR
1 TABLESPOON CORN-STARCH
1 CUP PINEAPPLE JUICE
1 TEASPOON VANILLA
1 TABLESPOON OLEOMAR-GARINE

a) Beat egg yolk. Add sugar, beating as you make the addition.
b) Mix cornstarch with pineapple juice, adding juice slowly to blend.

c) Add juice mixture to egg mixture. Mix. Add vanilla. Mix.
d) Cook in top of double boiler until thickened. About 10 to 15 minutes. Add oleomargarine and mix.
e) Cool filling.

11. Remove cakes from pans. Spread filling on top of 1 layer. Place second layer on top of filling.

Serves 12.

An excellent dessert or late party dessert with coffee.

VARIATIONS:
a) Use milk in place of pineapple juice for a cream filling.
b) Use orange juice in place of pineapple juice for an orange filling.

BLACKBERRY JAM CAKE

1 CUP BROWN SUGAR, PACKED
½ CUP OLEOMARGARINE
1 CUP BLACKBERRY JAM
1 CUP MASHED BANANAS (ABOUT 2 BANANAS)
2 CUPS SIFTED FLOUR
¼ TEASPOON CLOVES

¼ TEASPOON CINNAMON
¼ TEASPOON NUTMEG
1 TEASPOON BAKING POWDER
1 TEASPOON BAKING SODA
½ CUP BUTTERMILK
2 EGGS, WELL BEATEN
1 CUP CHOPPED NUTS

1. Cream sugar and oleomargarine.
2. Add jam and bananas. Mix well.
3. Sift flour with spices and baking powder. Sift again.
4. Mix baking soda with buttermilk.
5. Add flour alternately with buttermilk to the creamed mixture. Begin and end with some of the flour. Mix well.
6. Add eggs. Mix well.
7. Add nuts. Mix.
8. Pour into a well-greased 13 x 9 x 2 pan. Bake at 350° F. for 40 minutes.
9. Cool the cake. Dust with confectioners' sugar.

If you desire an icing on the Blackberry Jam Cake, I suggest the following:

3 CUPS SIFTED CONFEC-
TIONERS' SUGAR
¼ TEASPOON SALT
½ CUP MELTED OLEOMAR-
GARINE

          3 TABLESPOONS CREAM
          ½ TEASPOON VANILLA
          ½ TEASPOON LEMON EX-
              TRACT

1. Sift sugar with salt.
2. Add oleomargarine. Blend.
3. Add cream, vanilla, and lemon extract.
4. Beat all together until a creamy consistency. Spread.

DUXBURY CAKE

          1 CUP SUGAR
          ½ CUP SOFTENED OLEO-
              MARGARINE
          ½ CUP PEANUT BUTTER
          1½ CUPS SIFTED CAKE
              FLOUR
          2 TEASPOONS BAKING
              POWDER
          ¼ TEASPOON SALT
          2 MEDIUM BANANAS, CUT
              IN SLICES
          ¼ TEASPOON BAKING
              SODA MIXED WITH ½
              CUP BUTTERMILK
          1 TEASPOON VANILLA
          2 EGGS

1. Place all ingredients in an electric mixer.
2. Mix at slow speed until light and fluffy.
3. Bake in a well-greased 9 x 13 inch pan at 350° F. for 30 minutes.
4. Cool. Frost with the following icing:

4 CUPS SIFTED CONFEC-
TIONERS' SUGAR
2 TABLESPOONS CREAM
½ CUP MELTED OLEOMAR-
GARINE
1½ TEASPOONS BANANA
EXTRACT
1 CUP CHOPPED PEANUTS

a) Mix sugar and cream. Add oleomargarine. Mix.
b) Add extract. Beat until light and creamy.
c) Spread on cake and sprinkle with chopped nuts.

FUDGE CAKE

1 CUP OLEOMARGARINE
2 CUPS SUGAR
4 EGGS, WELL BEATEN
2 CUPS SIFTED CAKE
FLOUR
¼ TEASPOON SALT

1½ **TEASPOONS BAKING**
SODA
2/3 **CUP BUTTERMILK**
3 **SQUARES BITTER**
CHOCOLATE
2/3 **CUP BOILING WATER**
1 **TEASPOON VANILLA**

1. Cream oleomargarine and sugar.
2. Add eggs. Beat well.
3. Sift flour with salt. Mix soda with buttermilk. Add flour alternately with buttermilk to creamed mixture. Begin and end with some of the flour. Beat well.
4. Stir chocolate into boiling water to melt. Stir until smooth. While hot add to cake batter. Mix well.
5. Add vanilla. Beat well.
6. Bake in a well-greased 9 x 13 inch pan at 325° F. for 1 hour.
7. Cool cake and frost with Boiled Icing.
8. When icing is set, melt 2 squares of bitter chocolate and dribble or spread over top of boiled icing.

This cake is light and very rich.

Boiled Icing

2 CUPS SUGAR
½ CUP HOT WATER
2 EGG WHITES
1 TEASPOON VANILLA

1. Mix sugar with hot water in top of double boiler.
2. Add unbeaten egg whites. Beat with rotary egg beater or electric beater while mixture cooks. When frosting holds itself in peaks (about 10 minutes) remove from heat and beat in vanilla.
3. Spread icing.

HARLEQUIN CAKE

1 CUP OLEOMARGARINE
2 CUPS SUGAR
4 CUPS SIFTED CAKE FLOUR
5 TEASPOONS BAKING POWDER
1 1/3 CUPS MILK
2 TEASPOONS VANILLA
WHITES OF 6 EGGS (SAVE YOLKS FOR FILLING)
¼ TEASPOON RED FOOD COLORING

**½ TEASPOON YELLOW
FOOD COLORING
1 SQUARE BITTER
CHOCOLATE, MELTED**

1. Cream oleomargarine and sugar.
2. Sift flour with baking powder. Add alternately with milk to creamed mixture. Begin and end with some of the flour.
3. Add vanilla. Beat well.
4. Beat egg whites until stiff and fold into above mixture.
5. Divide batter into 4 parts. Color 1 part pink, 1 part yellow, add melted chocolate to 1 part and leave 1 part plain.
6. Place in 4 well-greased cake tins. Bake at 350° F. for 25 to 30 minutes. Cool.
7. Prepare the following lemon filling:

**1 CUP SUGAR
6 TABLESPOONS SIFTED
FLOUR
1½ TABLESPOONS CORN-
STARCH
¼ TEASPOON SALT
2½ CUPS WATER
6 EGG YOLKS, BEATEN
GRATED RIND OF 1
LEMON
JUICE OF 2 LEMONS**

a) Sift sugar with flour, cornstarch, and salt.
b) Add water gradually and mix well.
c) Place in top of double boiler. Cook 15 minutes. Stir to keep from lumping.
d) Add beaten egg yolks. Cook 3 minutes longer.
e) Add lemon juice and rind. Stir.
f) Add oleomargarine. Blend well.
g) Cool.

8. Place chocolate layer on bottom. Spread some filling. Top with yellow layer, more filling, pink layer, filling, and top with the plain layer of cake.
9. Spread top and sides with Boiled Icing (page 208).

Makes an excellent birthday cake.

PECAN DUST CAKE

1½ CUPS BROWN SUGAR, PACKED
½ CUP OLEOMARGARINE
3 EGGS, WELL BEATEN
2 CUPS SIFTED WHOLE-WHEAT FLOUR
½ CUP COFFEE
½ CUP COCOA
1 TEASPOON BAKING POWDER

⅛ TEASPOON SALT
1 TEASPOON SODA
¾ CUP BUTTERMILK
1 TEASPOON VANILLA

1. Cream sugar and oleomargarine well.
2. Add eggs and ½ cup of the flour. Mix well.
3. Heat coffee to a boil. Dissolve cocoa in hot coffee. Cool.
4. Sift remaining flour with baking powder and salt.
5. Mix soda with buttermilk.
6. Add flour with buttermilk to creamed mixture. Mix well.
7. Add cocoa mixture. Mix well.
8. Add vanilla. Mix.
9. Bake in a well-greased 9 x 13 x 2 inch pan at 350° F. for 30 to 35 minutes.
10. Cool. Top cake with the following icing:

½ CUP COCOA
3 CUPS CONFECTIONERS'
SUGAR
¼ CUP MELTED OLEOMAR-
GARINE
4 TABLESPOONS CREAM
1 TEASPOON VANILLA
¾ CUP FINELY CHOPPED
PECANS

a) Sift cocoa and sugar.

b) Add melted oleomargarine, cream, and vanilla.
c) Beat until creamy.
d) Spread on cake and sprinkle top with pecans.
Press nuts ever so slightly into icing.

The whole-wheat flour gives this cake an unusual
texture.

PINK HYACINTH CAKE

1 1 LB. CAN PURPLE
PLUMS
¾ CUP PLUM JUICE
½ CUP OLEOMARGARINE
1 CUP SUGAR
2 CUPS SIFTED CAKE
FLOUR
3 TEASPOONS BAKING
POWDER
½ TEASPOON SALT
⅛ TEASPOON RED FOOD
COLORING
3 EGG WHITES

1. Drain plums well. Save ¾ cup juice.
2. Pit plums and cut into very small pieces. Makes
1 cup.
3. Cream oleomargarine and sugar well.

4. Sift flour with baking powder and salt.
5. Add flour mixture alternately with the plum juice to creamed mixture. Begin and end with some of the flour. Beat well.
6. Add plums. Beat well.
7. Color batter a light pink color using the red food coloring.
8. Beat egg whites until stiff and fold into batter.
9. Pour batter into two well-greased and floured layer cake tins.
10. Bake at 350° F. for 30 to 35 minutes.
11. While cake is cooling make the following filling:

1 1 LB. CAN PURPLE PLUMS
2 TABLESOONS CORN-
STARCH

a) Drain plums. Mix plum juice with cornstarch.
b) Cook in top of double boiler until thickened and clear. Stir to prevent lumping.
c) Pit plums and cut into pieces. Add to thickened juice. Beat well to break up plum pieces.
d) Cool filling and spread between the 2 layers of cake.

12. Make Boiled Icing (page 208) and tint a delicate pink. Frost top and sides of cake.

This makes a colorful and delicious birthday cake.

PLUMNELLA CAKE

½ CUP OLEOMARGARINE
1½ CUPS BROWN SUGAR
4 EGGS, BEATEN
1 CUP COOKED PRUNES, MASHED
3 CUPS SIFTED CAKE FLOUR
3 TEASPOONS BAKING POWDER
1 TEASPOON BAKING SODA
½ TEASPOON SALT
1 CUP PRUNE JUICE

1. Cream oleomargarine and sugar.
2. Add eggs and prunes. Mix well.
3. Sift flour with baking powder, soda, and salt.
4. Add flour mixture alternately with prune juice. Begin and end with some of the flour. Mix well.
5. Bake in 2 well-greased layer cake pans at 375° F. for 30 to 40 minutes.
6. While cake is cooling make following filling:

1 CUP MILK
½ CUP SUGAR
2½ TABLESPOONS FLOUR
⅛ TEASPOON SALT

                    2 EGG YOLKS, WELL
                        BEATEN (SAVE WHITES
                        FOR FROSTING)
                    1½ TEASPOONS VANILLA

a) Scald milk in top of double boiler.
b) Mix sugar, flour, and salt. Add to milk stirring
   constantly. Cook until thickened, about 5
   minutes.
c) Add egg yolks and cook 3 minutes longer. Add
   vanilla.
d) Cool. Spread between the 2 layers.

7. Prepare the following frosting:

                    2 CUPS SUGAR
                    ½ CUP PRUNE JUICE
                    2 EGG WHITES
                    ½ TEASPOON VANILLA

a) Mix sugar and prune juice in top of double
   boiler.
b) Add egg whites.
c) Beat with rotary beater or electric beater as
   mixture cooks. When frosting holds itself in
   peaks as beater is lifted, remove from heat and
   beat in vanilla.
d) Spread over top and sides of cake.

ST. JOHNSBURY CAKE

½ CUP SUGAR
½ CUP OLEOMARGARINE
2 EGGS
½ CUP MAPLE SYRUP
2 CUPS SIFTED CAKE
FLOUR
¼ TEASPOON SALT
3 TEASPOONS BAKING
POWDER
¼ TEASPOON BAKING
SODA
1 CUP DATES, CUT UP
1/3 CUP MILK

1. Cream sugar and olemargarine.
2. Beat eggs until light. Add maple syrup. Beat well.
3. Add to the above and blend.
4. Sift flour with salt, baking powder, and soda.
5. Add half the flour to the creamed mixture. Mix well.
6. Mix dates with remaining flour. Add to the above with milk. Beat until well mixed.
7. Pour into a well-greased 9 x 13 inch pan. Bake at 350° F. for 25 to 30 minutes.
8. Cool. Ice with the following frosting:

1 CUP SUGAR
1 CUP MAPLE SYRUP

½ CUP MILK
⅛ TEASPOON SALT
2 TABLESPOONS OLEOMAR-
GARINE

1. Mix sugar, syrup, milk, and salt. Place over medium heat to boil. Stir well to dissolve sugar crystals as mixture comes to a boil. Cook until mixture forms a soft ball when a small amount is dropped into cold water.
2. Remove from heat and add oleomargarine. Do not stir. Allow icing to cool. Then beat for 10 or 12 minutes until it is the right consistency to spread on cake.

SUGAR AND SPICE AND EVERYTHING NICE

½ CUP OLEOMARGARINE
1 CUP BROWN SUGAR
2 EGGS, BEATEN
2 CUPS SIFTED WHOLE-
WHEAT FLOUR
½ TEASPOON CLOVES
1 TEASPOON CINNAMON
1 CUP RAISINS
1 TEASPOON BAKING SODA
1 CUP SOUR CREAM

1 LARGE RIPE BANANA
CUT IN CUBES

1. Cream oleomargarine and sugar.
2. Add eggs. Beat well.
3. Sift flour with spices. Add to the above mixture. Add raisins. Mix well.
4. Mix soda with sour cream. Add to the above. Mix well.
5. Add cubed banana. Mix well.
6. Bake in well-greased 9 x 12 inch pan at 350° F. for 30 minutes.
7. Remove from oven. While cake is still hot cover with the following frosting:

10 TABLESPOONS BROWN SUGAR
¼ LB. MELTED OLEOMAR-GARINE
1 CUP SHREDDED COCO-NUT

a) Mix brown sugar with melted oleomargarine.
b) Heat to the boiling point. Stir constantly.
c) Add shredded coconut. Mix well. Spread on cake immediately.
d) Place frosted cake under broiler to sizzle the icing and slightly brown coconut. About 2 minutes.

SUNKIST CAKE

½ CUP OLEOMARGARINE
1 CUP SUGAR
3 EGG YOLKS, BEATEN
GRATED RIND OF 2
ORANGES
2 CUPS SIFTED CAKE
FLOUR
½ TEASPOON SALT
3 TEASPOONS BAKING
POWDER
½ CUP ORANGE JUICE
3 EGG WHITES, BEATEN
STIFF
1 CUP CHOPPED CASHEW
NUTS

1. Cream oleomargine and sugar.
2. Add egg yolks and orange rind. Beat well.
3. Sift flour with salt and baking powder. Add alternately with orange juice to creamed mixture. Beat very well.
4. Fold in stiffly beaten egg whites.
5. Pour into 2 well-greased layer tins. Sprinkle chopped nuts over top of each layer.
6. Bake at 350° F. for 35 minutes.
7. Cool cakes and spread the following filling between layers:

219

½ CUP SUGAR
⅛ TEASPOON SALT
3½ TABLESPOONS CORN-
STARCH
1 2/3 CUPS ORANGE JUICE
2 EGG YOLKS, BEATEN
1 TABLESPOON OLEO-
MARGARINE
GRATED RIND OF 1
ORANGE

a) Mix sugar, salt, and cornstarch.
b) Add orange juice and stir until smooth.
c) Cook in a double boiler for 7 to 10 minutes, until thickened.
d) Add egg yolks and cook 3 minutes longer. Stirring during cooking process.
e) Remove from heat. Add oleomargarine and rind. Cool before spreading between layers.

8. Frost cake with following icing:

3 CUPS SIFTED CONFEC-
TIONERS' SUGAR
4 TABLESPOONS MELTED
OLEOMARGARINE
3 TABLESPOONS ORANGE
JUICE
SECTIONS OF 2 ORANGES

a) Beat confectioners' sugar, oleomargarine, and orange juice until smooth and creamy.

b) Spread over top and sides of cake.

c) Arrange orange sections on top of cake to form a pleasing design. Orange sections are to be free of seeds and membrane.

Serves 10 to 12.

A dash of whipped cream adds to the richness of the cake.

WATERMELON CAKE

1 CUP SUGAR

½ CUP OLEOMARGARINE

3 EGG YOLKS AND 2 EGG WHITES (SAVE THE OTHER EGG WHITE FOR ICING)

¼ TEASPOON RED FOOD COLORING

2 CUPS SIFTED CAKE FLOUR

3 TEASPOONS BAKING POWDER

¼ TEASPOON SALT

½ CUP MILK

**3 TABLESPOON LEMON
JUICE
COARSELY GRATED RIND
OF 2 LEMONS
¼ CUP POPPY SEEDS**

1. Cream sugar and oleomargarine.
2. Beat egg yolks and egg whites until light. Add coloring. Mix.
3. Add egg mixture to creamed mixture. Mix.
4. Sift flour with baking powder and salt.
5. Add flour and milk alternately to creamed mixture. Beat well.
6. Add lemon juice and rind. Mix.
7. Spread half the batter in a well-greased 4½ x 13 inch loaf pan. Pour poppy seeds down the center, lengthwise, of batter to form the melon seeds. Cover with remaining batter.
8. Bake at 350° F. for 40 to 45 minutes.
9. Cool cake. Remove to serving plate and frost entire cake with Boiled Frosting (page 208) tinted a delicate green.

5. Invert cake on a cake rack to cool.
6. Remove from pan and split into three horizontal slices.
7. Fill with this filling:

> 5 TABLESPOONS FLOUR
> 1 CUP SUGAR
> 5 TABLESPOONS COCOA
> ¼ TEASPOON SALT
> ½ CUP CREAM
> 1½ CUPS COFFEE
> 3 EGGS OR 5 YOLKS, BEATEN WELL
> 1 TEASPOON VANILLA

a) Sift flour, sugar, cocoa, and salt together.
b) Add coffee and cream. Mix well.
c) Cook in top of double boiler for 10 minutes. Add eggs and cook for 3 minutes.
d) Add vanilla. Cool filling before spreading between cake layers.

8. Frost with this icing:

> ½ CUP COCOA
> 3 CUPS CONFECTIONERS' SUGAR
> 1¼ CUPS WHIPPED CREAM
> 1 TEASPOON VANILLA
> 1 CUP CHOPPED, TOASTED HAZELNUTS

a) Sift sugar and cocoa together.
b) Add whipped cream. Blend and beat well until butter cream consistency. Add vanilla.

9. Frost the top and sides of cake.
10. Sprinkle with 1 cup chopped, toasted hazelnuts over the entire cake.

Elegant and delicious bridge party dessert or for special company. One could use a large bakery angel food cake and short-cut the first part of the recipe.

Serves 12 to 16, depending on size of servings and for which purpose intended. Just after dinner dessert, perhaps 18 servings.

NOTES

NOTES

PIES

CHERRY MERINGUE PIE

1 UNBAKED PIE SHELL
3 EGGS, SEPARATED
½ TEASPOON ALMOND EXTRACT
¼ CUP MELTED OLEOMARGARINE
1 CUP SUGAR
¼ CUP FLOUR
⅛ TEASPOON SALT
4 CUPS SOUR CHERRIES (2 1 LB. CANS IN WATER PACK)

1. Beat egg yolks. Add extract and oleomargarine. Mix.
2. Sift sugar with flour and salt. Toss drained cherries in flour mixture.
3. Mix egg mixture with the cherries. Fill pie shell.
4. Bake at 375° F. for 45 minutes or until set.
5. Remove pie from oven and top with the following meringue:
   a) Beat 3 egg whites until frothy stiff.
   b) Add 9 tablespoons sugar. Beat as you add the sugar.
   c) Add 1 teaspoon vinegar and beat until the meringue holds itself in peaks. Spread on pie.
6. Bake at 350° F. for 15 minutes longer.
   Serves 6.

232

CHESS FRUIT PIE

1 CUP BROWN SUGAR
½ CUP OLEOMARGARINE
½ CUP CREAM
3 WHOLE EGGS AND 1 YOLK
1 CUP CHOPPED ENGLISH WALNUTS
1 CUP RAISINS
1 TEASPOON VANILLA
1 TEASPOON LEMON RIND
1 TEASPOON LEMON JUICE
1 EGG WHITE, STIFFLY BEATEN
2 TABLESPOONS WHITE SUGAR
1 UNBAKED PIE SHELL

1. Cream sugar and oleomargarine.
2. Add cream. Mix well.
3. Add eggs and yolk, one at a time, beating well after each addition.
4. Add nuts, raisins, vanilla, lemon rind, and lemon juice. Mix well.
5. Beat white sugar into stiffly beaten egg white and fold into above mixture.
6. Pour into pie shell and bake at 350° F. for 40 minutes or until set.

Serve with a dash of whipped cream.

DATE PIE

1 LB. DATES
1 CUP WATER
2 TABLESPOONS SUGAR
¼ TEASPOON CINNAMON
¼ TEASPOON GINGER
¼ TEASPOON SALT
1 TABLESPOON LEMON
   JUICE
3 EGGS, BEATEN
2 CUPS MILK
1 UNBAKED PIE SHELL

1. Cook dates slowly in 1 cup of water for 20 minutes.
2. Sift sugar, cinnamon, ginger, and salt together. Add to dates with lemon juice. Mix well.
3. Mix eggs and milk. Add to date mixture. Stir.
4. Pour into pie shell and bake at 375° F. for 50 minutes.
5. Serve with whipped cream.

Serves 8.

FRESH RHUBARB PIE

1 UNBAKED PIE SHELL
AND TOP CRUST
5 CUPS FRESH RHUBARB,
CUT IN PIECES (ABOUT
2 LBS.)
1 CUP SUGAR
1 TABLESPOON FLOUR
2 EGGS, BEATEN
1½ TABLESPOONS BUTTER

1. Sift sugar with flour. Mix well with rhubarb.
2. Pour into pie shell. Pour eggs over rhubarb. Dot with butter.
3. Cover with top crust and prick a few holes with a fork. Brush with a little cream.
4. Bake at 425° F. for 10 minutes. Reduce heat to 350° F. for 50 minutes.

A serving of hard sauce would be tasty with this pie.

Serves 8.

FRESH STRAWBERRY GLACÉ PIE

1 BAKED PIE SHELL
1 QUART FRESH STRAW-
BERRIES
1 CUP SUGAR
2 CUPS MILK
¾ CUP SUGAR
5 TABLESPOONS FLOUR
¼ TEASPOON SALT
4 EGG YOLKS, BEATEN
1 TEASPOON VANILLA
2½ TABLESPOONS CORN-
STARCH
1 TABLESPOON FLOUR
1 TABLESPOON BUTTER

1. Wash and cap berries. Cut in halves. Mix with 1 cup sugar. Allow to stand 1 hour.
2. Scald milk in double boiler.
3. Sift sugar with flour and salt. Add to milk. Cook for 15 minutes.
4. Add egg yolks. Cook 3 minutes longer.
5. Add vanilla. Cool until warm and pour into pie shell.
6. Drain berries. There should be 1½ cups of juice. Add orange juice if needed to make this amount.
7. Sift cornstarch and 1 tablespoon flour. Add juice stirring to make smooth. Cook in double boiler

until thickened and somewhat transparent. Add butter. Mix.

8. Fold strawberries into sauce and spread over the top of pie.
9. Refrigerate before serving. A dash of whipped cream is best on the pie.

Serves 8.

GOOSEBERRY PIE

1 UNBAKED PIE SHELL AND TOP CRUST
1 NO. 303 1 LB. CAN GOOSEBERRIES IN HEAVY SYRUP
1¼ CUPS SUGAR
5 TABLESPOONS CORN-STARCH
2 TABLESPOONS OLEO-MARGARINE
½ CUP ORANGE MARMA-LADE

1. Drain berries. Mix juice with ¾ cup sugar and cornstarch.
2. Place in top of double boiler and cook 15 minutes. Stir to prevent lumping.
3. Remove from heat. Add oleomargarine, berries,

237

½ cup sugar, and marmalade. Mix together and pour into pie shell.

4. Cover with top crust. Make a few slits in top crust to allow steam to escape during baking process.
5. Bake at 400° F. for 40 minutes.
6. Cool pie and serve with a dash of Old English Hard Sauce (page 183).

Serves 8.

HOT BUTTER BLACK RASPBERRY PIE

1 UNBAKED PIE SHELL AND TOP CRUST
2 CANS 15 OZ. SIZE BLACK RASPBERRIES
6 TABLESPOONS CORN-STARCH
1½ CUPS SUGAR
¼ TEASPOON SALT
2 TABLESPOONS BUTTER

TOPPING
8 TEASPOONS SOFT BUTTER
8 TEASPOONS SUGAR

OLD-FASHIONED
CHOCOLATE CREAM PIE

1 BAKED PIE SHELL
5 TABLESPOONS FLOUR
1 CUP SUGAR
⅛ TEASPOON SALT
5 TABLESPOONS COCOA
2 CUPS MILK
3 EGGS, SEPARATED
¼ LB. OLEOMARGARINE
1 TEASPOON VANILLA

1. Sift flour with sugar, salt, and cocoa.
2. Add milk. Stir until smooth.
3. Place in double boiler and cook for 12 minutes. Stir to prevent lumping.
4. Beat egg yolks. Add to the above mixture and cook for 3 minutes. Stir often. A wire whip is helpful for the stirring process.
5. Remove from fire and add oleomargarine and vanilla. Mix. Cool slightly and pour into pie shell.
6. Spread with the following meringue:
   a) Beat 3 egg whites until frothy stiff.
   b) Add 9 tablespoons sugar. Beat as you add the sugar.
   c) Add ½ teaspoon vinegar and beat until the meringue holds itself in peaks. Spread on pie.
7. Bake at 375° F. for 12 minutes.

This makes a 9 inch pie. 4 egg whites will make a higher meringue.

Add 3 tablespoons sugar for each egg white added.

PUMPKIN PIE ROYAL

1 UNBAKED PIE SHELL
1 CUP SCALDED MILK
1 TABLESPOON OLEOMAR-
  GARINE
¾ CUP COOKED OR
  CANNED PUMPKIN
½ CUP BROWN SUGAR
¼ CUP WHITE SUGAR
¼ TEASPOON SALT
½ TEASPOON CINNAMON
½ TEASPOON NUTMEG
⅛ TEASPOON CLOVES
2 EGGS, BEATEN

1. Add oleomargarine to scalded milk.
2. Mix pumpkin, sugars, salt, and spices. Stir into the above.
3. Add eggs. Mix.
4. Pour into pie shell.
5. Bake at 375° F. for 45 minutes.
6. Remove from oven and cool.
7. Prepare the following cream filling:

1 CUP MILK
¼ CUP SUGAR
2½ TABLESPOONS FLOUR
⅛ TEASPOON SALT
2 EGG YOLKS, BEATEN
½ TEASPOON VANILLA

a) Scald milk in top of double boiler.
b) Mix sugar, flour, and salt. Add to milk. Stir well and cook for 15 minutes.
c) Add egg yolks. Stir and cook 5 minutes.
d) Add vanilla. Mix.
e) Pour over pumpkin filling.

8. Prepare the following meringue:

4 EGG WHITES (USE 2 LEFT FROM ABOVE)
¾ CUP SUGAR
1 TEASPOON VINEGAR

a) Beat egg whites until stiff.
b) Add sugar gradually while beating.
c) Add vinegar and continue to beat until meringue stands in peaks.
d) Spread over top of cream filling.

9. Bake pie at 350° F. for 15 minutes.

For a good old-fashioned rich pumpkin pie—without the cream filling and meringue—use 1½ times the recipe for the pumpkin filling and follow steps 1 through 6.

SAIGON CHOCOLATE PIE

CRUST

> 2 CUPS FINE GRAHAM CRACKER CRUMBS
> ¼ TEASPOON CINNAMON
> ¼ CUP MELTED OLEOMARGARINE

FILLING

> 1 CUP MILK
> 2 SQUARES GRATED CHOCOLATE
> 1 TABLESPOON SIFTED FLOUR
> ¼ TEASPOON SALT
> 1 CUP SUGAR
> 2 EGGS, BEATEN
> ½ TEASPOON VANILLA

1. Mix crumbs with cinnamon. Add oleomargarine and blend together with fingers. Press evenly over the bottom and sides of a pie pan.
2. Heat milk and chocolate in double boiler. Mix as chocolate melts.
3. Sift flour with salt and sugar. Add to milk. Stir with wire whip to mix well. Remove from heat.
4. Add eggs and vanilla. Mix.
5. Pour filling into pie shell. Bake at 375° F. for 50 minutes.

6. Serve with 1 cup whipped cream mixed with 2 tablespoons sugar and ¼ teaspoon cinnamon.

Serves 6.

SATIN PIE

CRUST

2 CUPS CLUB CRACKER CRUMBS
1 CUP FINELY CHOPPED PECANS
½ CUP MELTED BUTTER

1. Roll the cracker crumbs fine. Mix with the chopped nuts.
2. Add the melted butter and blend.
3. Place in a 10 inch pie tin and press to form a pie crust. Bake at 375° F. for 10 minutes. Cool.
4. Prepare the following filling:

¾ CUP BUTTER
1 CUP EXTRA FINE DESSERT SUGAR
¾ CUP COCOA
4 EGGS
1 TEASPOON VANILLA
½ TEASPOON ALMOND EXTRACT

247

a) Place butter in an electric mixer and whip.

b) Sift sugar and cocoa. Add slowly to the whipped butter on low speed. Increase speed as mixture is blended. If mixture is too stiff add 1 egg and continue beating.

c) Add the eggs, one at a time, beating well to blend after each addition.

d) Whip on high speed until the consistency of whipped cream. Add vanilla and almond extract and blend.

e) Pour mixture into baked shell and place in refrigerator to set about 1 ½ to 2 hours.

f) Cut and serve with whipped cream to which chopped maraschino cherries have been added. Use ¼ cup chopped cherries to 1 cup of whipped cream.

Superbly rich. Serves 10 for a dessert or 8 servings for a beverage and dessert party.

This pie may also be made by using a regular baked pie shell and sprinkling chopped nuts over the top before placing in refrigerator.

NOTES

NOTES

NOTES

NOTES

INDEX